When You Walk A Dark Valley

By
Ellen Dana

TEACH Services, Inc.
www.TEACHServices.com

Copyright © 2007 TEACH Services, Inc.
ISBN-13: 978-1-57258-477-8
Library of Congress Control Number: 2007927797

Published by
TEACH Services, Inc.
www.TEACHServices.com

CONTENTS

Preface.. *v*

Introduction ....*vii*

As You Begin Your Study.....................................*ix*

Lesson 1 Count It All Joy.. 1
In Every Circumstance
Daily Log
Daily Log—sample

Lesson 2 Retraining Your Thoughts 17
To Safeguard Your Imagination

Lesson 3 Escape From Bitterness 29
Finding Escape Tools That Work

Lesson 4 When Forgiveness Seems Too Difficult— 45
You Need A Heart

Lesson 5 Throwing Off the Spirit of Heaviness To Receive His .. 59
Garment of Praise

The Awesome Truth About God's Fire.......................... 65
A Bible Study

PREFACE

Traffic was only moderate as my car sped through the dark night. While my three teenagers slept away the miles in the back of our station wagon my mind churned with the events of the last few days, and then wandered back to the last few weeks. The memories were so horrifying and bizarre that I could barely grasp their reality. Worst of all, I knew of no one with whom I could discuss those events.

Yes, I was a Christian, and yes, I could pray. I had prayed through each unreal happening. But I had never read anything similar to this, I had never heard anyone discuss such situations being even a possibility. I was floored and I was numb. Most of all I felt an incredible aloneness. I decided my present state was worse than being left alone on a desert island in the midst of the vast Pacific Ocean.

"What I wouldn't give for a human being to notice that I'm breathing on planet earth," I mused. "Even if a cop pulled me over right now—at least I would know that my life matters in some way to somebody!" I shook my head and cracked the window, letting the cool night air rush full blast against my sleepy head. A few minutes later I turned at my exit and slowed my pace through sleepy downtown streets. Not much traffic at 1 a.m.

I drove through town, and into the country for the last few miles to home. Suddenly, red lights flashed behind me. My desperate inner cry had not gone unnoticed by my Friend Jesus! The state patrolman was kind, only wondering if I was OK. He had seen my car weaving clear back on the Interstate. He noticed my teenage kids asleep in the back of the car, and learned that my home was just around the corner ahead. Satisfying himself that I was merely very tired, he waved me on. "My wife and kids are out on the road tonight, too," he said. He never knew how God used him that night to answer my cry for a human being to care that I existed. No, it was not on a personal level; he was only doing his job. But it was enough; it *was* a personal gift from my God, for I knew *He* had not forgotten me as I stumbled through this incomprehensible journey—a journey that I was forced to believe because the facts glared in my face.

Why do I share this glimpse of my past without telling you the rest of the story? I tell you because you may be in a similar situation at this moment, struggling to maintain a semblance of sanity in an insane world. When those around you become caught up in any one of the many snares set for them by the enemy of our souls, someone else suffers. Sometimes we are the victims of the hold that Satan has on those who are "significant others" in our lives. I've been there; in fact, I've been there more than I can count. I tell you this because I want you to know that I understand the pain that may threaten you, as well. I also want you to know that in the depths of the darkness that seems almost to obliterate the path before your feet, a light is burning. *Look for it*, not at the end of the tunnel, *but at your very feet, for our God reminds us,* "*Thy Word is a lamp unto my feet and a light unto my path.*" **Psalm 119:105**

My prayer is that you will take each promise as your own and let these precious gleams grow stronger as the days go by.

I am simply your fellow traveler on this speck of a planet in the universe. I do not need to know all the details of your life, or your present dark valley. May God's love bring the strength that comes from knowing we have a Savior who is in control when everything around us appears to have crashed in shambles. Let the true, unchanging principles in God's Word empower you for the pilgrimage of your life and there find *meaningful life*, even life to *possess "more abundantly."*

—Ellen Dana, Bible Educator

INTRODUCTION

This book is the culmination of learning from God's Word applied to experiences of many years. Disappointments and heartache brought discouragement and despair, until I learned they came from the Master's hand. Little by little I learned to trust Him and to surrender to His wisdom and unfailing love. Only years later, did I notice this Scripture:

"Blessed is the man whose strength is in thee; in whose heart are the ways of them. Who passing through the valley of Baca make it a well; the rain also filled the pools. They go from strength to strength, everyone of them in Zion appeareth before God." (Psalms 84:5-7).

I learned that Baca is a troublesome plant growing in a valley in the Middle East. It catches the clothing and makes the traveler's way through this valley treacherous and wearisome. I soon saw the spiritual application. Those who traverse life's road do not choose that lonely, "dark valley" route, and often find they have arrived at its edge unexpectedly. Surprised at how they came to this loathsome spot, they scan the horizon hoping to see the slope of some "delectable mountain" of unbounded joy where again will ring the gladsome sound and warmth of human companionship. They look not for the senseless mirth of the careless crowd, but the sweet joy of spiritual and intellectual bonding with likeminded souls.

The Psalmist knew of the literal valley—a lonely stretch of land and the troublesome Baca plant. Yet he said, "Blessed the "man whose strength is in Thee (in God), in whose heart are the ways of them." (Psalms 84:5). Whose heart? Evidently the hearts of prior travelers through this "valley of weeping." Many Christians realize that we can expect financial struggles, and we cannot escape all physical and emotional pain; they are as legacies from Adam to all who come from his loins. Sickness, slander or misunderstanding and rejection by friends all dot the landscape of this frightful Valley of Baca. But this lonely valley portion, unexpected as it is, is neither recognized at first glance as a portion of the valley of Baca, nor valued as a place that produces strength.

What makes this lonely ordeal of surprising value? "They (the former travelers) passing through, *make it a well; the rain also filleth the pools.*" (verse 6).

So here is its secret! Rain—that blessed sprinkling that denotes an unbreakable bond with the Father, fills the pools. Though our tears may flow, this rain is not the tears, but rather *it is His precious raining Holy Spirit that fills the wells* in this lonely Valley of Baca. Those who have traveled the dark, lonely valley for a long time may never have chosen it for themselves, but *they have learned to embrace it.* As you stoop to drink at each well—each comfort of His Spirit—may He ravish your heart with the love of Jesus until your life is filled with heaven's light and joy. You will then experience with the Psalmist...

"They go from strength to strength; everyone of them in Zion appeareth (is seen and regarded) before God" (Psalms 84:7). You will be prepared to leave personal wells of blessing in your lonely valley for those who come after you. All praise to the Father and His precious Son—our Friend and Comfort no matter how dark the journey.

AS YOU BEGIN YOUR STUDY

The focus of this short mind-management course is to help those who are only trudging through life, barely surviving emotionally, rather than thriving in the atmosphere of heaven. Some may be headed for depression unless they find God's answers now while turning attitudes, moods and wrong thinking habits around by His power and grace.

We need to remind ourselves however, that your brain is a part of your body for brain and body do not operate independently of one another. As important as mind management is, please do not be misled into thinking that proper mind management alone will always resolve all your troubles completely. The way you care for and feed your body will have a profound effect on how you operate your mind and how well it is able to function.

For this reason, I encourage you to consider looking at possible physical improvements you should put into effect. Look for those who advocate the 8 basic laws of health, sometimes called the "8 natural doctors." The names of those doctors are sunshine, fresh air, proper nutrition, temperance, rest, exercise and trust in divine power. Mental struggles become much easier to manage, and some even disappear completely when those 8 doctors are consulted, and heeded. A little thing like drinking at least 8 glasses of water a day (not pop or other polluted liquids), will give the brain adequate cleansing and refreshment. Since the brain is made up of about 75% water, be sure to provide plenty of this amazing liquid. A daily brisk walk in fresh air, while you thank God for the beauties of His creation you will be accessing another free "doctor" who will bring refreshment to your mind, soul and body.

If you've been living on grease-filled "fast foods" with little to no fresh vegetables and fruits, your body, and thus your brain, may be starving for good nutrition. Consider eating more fresh foods, while you decrease or eliminate flesh foods, with nothing between meals.

Why is all this so important? Because you have an enemy who works even through what *you* eat and drink as well. Even through your eating and drinking habits? Yes!

Does that sound far-fetched? It has been shown over and over that caffeine, for example, causes people to quickly "short-circuit" and "blow a fuse" over little annoyances. You probably know folks like this, people who intellectually know better and may even want to do better, yet continually hurt those they profess to love the most, yell at those who do them good, and rage at other drivers on the road—even those who remain unconscious of their supposed outright selfishness at "cutting in front" of someone

These are simply examples of health improvements that would also help your mind to function better. To fully develop these principles is beyond the scope of this book, but we want to alert you that changes in health habits are necessary and will have significant impact on your ability to handle life's challenges.

Lesson 1

COUNT IT ALL JOY

IN EVERY CIRCUMSTANCE

Cynthia could not think of much that should bring happiness and joy to her life. Instead, she was a very unhappy wife expecting her second child, but planning to move out. She had arranged a job and childcare in another city but being raised in a church that is not favorable to divorce, she knew that she did not have grounds for such action. Only guilt was keeping her at home.

Cynthia describes her pitiful condition: "It had been some time since I had prayed. The cares of this life had taken the place of God in my life. Building a house and then keeping it along with caring for our toddler occupied my hours. But my mind was occupied in disagreeable thoughts about my husband. I certainly had reasons for complaints. He worked all the time rising early and coming home late. He took off very little time for the family. In his mind providing for his family materially was demonstrating his love but I longed for other demonstrations.

"Finally one night I cried out to God in desperation. I told Him just how miserable I was and how much I wanted out of this relationship but that I knew it was not right in His eyes for me to leave. I begged for help. I thought that help would have to be a major change in my husband. I told God many things about my husband that needed changing. Finally I was quiet and God spoke to me."

Now what do you suppose God told Cynthia? Did He agree with her felt need to see changes in her husband? Did He whisper, "I don't blame you for feeling as you do?"

It was neither of these. God had a surprise for Cynthia and moreover there was never any question in her mind that it really was God talking, and not some ramblings of her own thoughts:

> I know that it was God speaking to me because the thoughts were totally foreign to anything that I would or could have imagined on my own. God gave me very specific instructions that if followed would bring healing. He told me to get a sheet of paper and write out 10 things that I liked about my husband and to keep that paper in my pocket and when I was tempted to think the negative thoughts that constantly filled my mind about my husband I was to take out that paper and review those 10 points. I went to sleep at peace.
>
> The next morning I awoke knowing what I needed to do. When I had some quiet time I sat down with paper and pen and started to write, but no good things came to mind. It took me hours that day to jot down 10 good things about my husband. I could have written pages of changes that I wanted to see in him but this assignment was much harder. However, I KNEW that these instructions were straight from God and I worked to fulfill the assignment.

What was the result of Cynthia's prescription from heaven? We'll return to her story in a moment, but first, let me ask you, Are you experiencing circumstances that have resulted in similar negative thinking patterns? Would you describe yourself as fearful, lonely, forgotten, stressed, unfairly treated, shamed, sick or in pain? Have your thoughts led you to feelings of sadness and despair that result in a minimal survival mode? This is your opportunity to consider your own emotional climate—but only long enough to prepare for healing of heart and soul.

The feelings you experience likely began with events that triggered wrong thoughts. In other words, it is likely that something went on in your mind when a real or perceived negative episode, or ongoing actions of others struck your mind as being against you. You began to harbor hurt, woeful feelings. Contrary to popular belief, feelings come **after** your thoughts, not before! The good news is that you can resolve wrong thinking patterns and in so doing, your feelings will dramatically change. Let's explore some of the possible thought patterns.

A. Prolonged, overwhelming sadness—When a loved one dies, it is natural to be sad—to feel that you are walking through a dark tunnel of despair. That grief needs an outlet and God provided the means—tears. To bottle up your emotions at this stage and refrain from crying would not be healthful or helpful. However, to continue crying for months works against you. Even at funerals today many are taking the time to remember the good things about the individual, the happy times together, the specialness of this one who is no longer with them. If you make it a habit to use your mind in this way, and then look for ways to continue the thoughtfulness and beauty of the life that is no longer with you by ministering that spirit to others, you will be lifted up and away from continuing grief.

B. Unrealistic expectations of others—Some may try to place too much responsibility on other people. For example, a woman may marry, thinking that her "Prince Charming," will make her happy, bending to her every whim and desire. His inability or his resistance to the idea of catering to her many whims *or even to her logical needs*, can disappoint and anger such a woman, if she does not choose to face reality.

C. Disobedience to God's revealed will—God's laws, whether it is the Ten Commandment moral code, or a law of physics, are fixed and certain. No scientist would question the law of gravity. Although the scientist does not know what it is, he knows and experiences the reality of this powerful force. He would not think of working on the outside of the tenth floor of a downtown office building without some safety measures to protect him from falling. The prisons are full of people who disregarded the law that says, "Thou shalt not steal," or "Thou shalt not kill," because society will not tolerate those who ignore their right to enjoy their own belongings. Like a stagnant pond without an outlet, neither does it bring life to an individual who is continually receiving but never giving to others.

D. Shame and Distress caused by actions of significant people in our lives. These kinds of dark days are much harder than death to manage. For example, if a spouse chooses to cherish another lover, or succumbs to evil habits, even becoming a child molester, perhaps as the result of an addiction to pornography, it may take some time to find a mechanism for coping with this reality that seems to contain no remnant of realism, no hope of remedy. But even out of a horrific situation such as this, God can bring a miracle beyond what you ever thought possible.

E. Financial reversals or physical pain and illness. Even in these, God can become closer and more real than when good things happen to you.

F. Thoughtless, insensitive remarks or berating judgments from people who think to "bring you to repentance" for some supposed "sin" in your life—wounding rather than wooing you closer to Jesus as the Savior Himself would do.

Is it possible for you to develop trust and positive, joyful living while dealing with one or more of the above heartaches or physical stress? Yes, it is! You may begin to practice this "joyful walk," through working in harmony with right laws that govern your mind and how it works.

Let's see what happened to Cynthia when she allowed God to speak to her heart.

"Over the coming days I had to pull that paper from my pocket very often as negative thoughts were so ingrained in my thinking. But I also found that I had to do other things to prevent those unhappy thoughts. I discovered that the music that I was listening to was contributing to my unhappiness. The rock and country songs that told the stories of unhappy people who found consolation outside of their marriage relationships were not planting helpful thoughts to repairing my marriage. Somehow that obvious fact had escaped my notice before. I destroyed those records and turned off the radio."

And what was the result?

"In the space of 3 months I was happy again and my husband was nicer too. Obviously, my negativity had influenced him and now my happier outlook had an affect on him as well. We began to enjoy sweet times. Best of all, I began a walk with God that filled me with wonder and joy.

"It would be years before my husband would learn to take time for family. I would raise the children with less input from him than I would have liked, but gradually he did take more time and his walk with the Lord blossomed. We thank the Lord daily for our family and for His saving power."

Did you know that the Father is interested in your circumstances as well? Whether your troubles have developed largely by wrong thinking patterns as in Cynthia's case, or instead, as a result of the actions of a significant person in your life who is very cruel. He understands. He has seen your tears and your despair.

Your pains might come from one or more of the common stressors of life listed below— wounds we mentioned briefly back on page three. Right now, check in your mind (since it is best to keep your list private!) the following feelings that apply to you personally:

1. Guilt or fear
2. Great loneliness, ill or weak
3. Disappointed, abandoned and forgotten
4. Deep emotional shame
5. Extreme stress
6. Very unfairly treated
7. In pain and sickness

Even if you do not have a husband or wife to minister the Savior's love to you by speaking tenderly to you of God's love and devotion, at this moment *you may nestle in the arms of our heavenly Father without the aid of a human arm.* The following prayer is given and anointed by the Holy Spirit to speak to you personally. Please allow that sweet heavenly Spirit of God to minister this prayer to your heart:

My prayer for you:
"Father, I pray just now for _____, who is experiencing circumstances listed above, or possible others, as likely causes for his/her feelings of despair and hopelessness. I ask for Your Holy Spirit to come in to minister mightily in his/her behalf. Thank you for Your Word of hope and promise. May this wounded, tired heart be carried to Your bosom and there find healing of heart and mind. May a strong bond of intimate fellowship begin and continue developing with

You, a bond that cannot be broken. In the precious name of Your Son, Jesus Christ, Who died so that _____ can now experience Your love first hand," Amen.

In each of these specific hurts, God wants to give you His Son—His gift to you—all of His treasure Who came for you in human form. Jesus will become complete healing to you. Receiving all of Jesus means that...

- It will no longer be necessary for you to cling to the pains caused by thoughtless or unkind significant others in your life
- You will not need to remain chained to old ways of thinking about the negatives of the past and the present.
- You will discover that it is possible to experience freedom from emotional pain and ability to handle physical distress.
- You will glorify God by finding the freedom that our loving Father wants to bring You. You will be enabled to demonstrate the love, compassion and tenderness of Jesus and His Father, and thus to make Him manifest to the world.

To you, right now, you are receiving "Jesus, who is made unto us wisdom, righteousness, sanctification and redemption." (1 Corinthians 1:30).

What does that mean? As you receive Him, He encompasses that promise and details the specifics of what He waits to give you through His "great and precious promises." (2 Peter 1:4.).

Your focus may have been on your struggles, your pain, or some unjust treatment. Now turn your focus to the One Who understands whatever you are experiencing. Take this paragraph as yours

"Often your mind may be clouded because of pain. Then do not try to think. You know that Jesus loves you. He understands your weakness. You may do His will by simply resting in His arms." E. White in *Ministry of Healing,* page 251.

Did you mentally check number one on page 5 because you've been feeling full of guilt or fearfulness? Yes, Jesus is made unto us wisdom... and He says, "Say to them that are of a fearful heart, Be strong, fear not: behold, your God will come with vengeance, even God with a recompense; He will come and save you." (Isaiah 35:4). Receiving Jesus means that you have received His love. Do you know what love does? "Perfect love casteth out fear." (1 John 4:18).

If you checked number two because you've been experiencing great loneliness or weakness, then "Jesus is made unto us wisdom..." and while on earth, as well as today, He said, "Come unto me, all ye that labor and are heavy laden, and I will give you rest." (Matthew 11:28.)

Have you felt abandoned and forgotten lately and that's why you checked number three? Remember that "Jesus is made unto us wisdom and righteousness and sanctification and redemption." That's everything friend, but to be even more specific, think of this—"But if from thence thou shalt seek the LORD thy God, *thou shalt find him*, if thou seek him with all thy heart and with all thy soul. When thou art in tribulation, and all these things are come upon thee, even in the latter days, if thou turn to the LORD thy God, and shalt be obedient unto his voice; (For the LORD thy God is a merciful God;) He will not forsake thee, neither destroy thee, nor forget the covenant of thy fathers which he sware unto them." (Deuteronomy 4:29–31).

If you checked number four which says you have experienced great emotional and devastating shame, again, Jesus is made unto us wisdom and righteousness (and if He is righteousness to us, the shame has been eradicated; perhaps it's time to trust that this is really so!) Trusting means believing what He says is true for you. Jeremiah says it well, "Blessed is the man that trusteth in the LORD, and whose hope the LORD is." (Jeremiah 17:7).

If you've been stressed and pressured at home, at work, or even at church, you probably checked number five mentally. Much of stress and pressure is accepted if we don't know how to handle our work load or our daily schedule. Whatever the situation, "Jesus is made unto us, wisdom...!"

Have you thanked the Lord for that? And have you thanked Him and chosen to accept this promise? "Great peace have they which love Thy law, and nothing shall offend them."

You checked number six if you've been feeling unfairly treated. That feeling is not easily put aside with your "natural man" nature—called "carnal." But don't forget that Jesus was made unto us wisdom, and righteousness and (even) sanctification (with His perfect, divine nature) in place of your carnal nature. If you accept His sanctification, *He will remove the feeling,* for His nature harbors no bitterness, wrath or anger. It will be easy then to claim His promise to "Let all bitterness, and wrath, and anger, and clamor, and evil speaking, be put away from you, with all malice: And be ye kind one to another, tenderhearted, forgiving one another, even as God for Christ's sake hath forgiven you." (Ephesians 4:31, 32).

If you've been plagued with pain and sickness, you surely checked number seven. You are grateful that He has promised that "...God shall wipe away all tears from their eyes; and there shall be no more death, neither sorrow, nor crying, neither shall there be any more pain: for the former things are passed away." (Revelation 21:4). You recognize that if you have allowed Jesus to be made all that there is in 1 Corinthians 1:30, you can wait for that day when this will all be true.

What is the result of receiving this promise and rejoicing that soon there will be no more pain or sorrow? "He crowneth thee with lovingkindness and tender mercies." You have just been crowned as a king to reign with Christ right now— to rule over your own spirit, and to represent the King of the universe to those around you! He is now enabling you to give glory to God—to show and minister His character to your portion of this dark world. (Exodus 19:6; Revelation 5:10; 1 Thessalonians 2:12)

"The spirit of the Lord GOD is upon me; because the LORD hath anointed me to preach good tidings unto the meek; he hath sent me to bind up the brokenhearted, to proclaim liberty to the captives, and the opening of the prison to them that are bound; To proclaim the acceptable year of the LORD, and the day of vengeance of our God; to comfort all that mourn; To appoint unto them that mourn in Zion, to give unto them beauty for ashes, the oil of joy for mourning, the garment of praise for the spirit of heaviness; that they might be called trees of righteousness, the planting of the LORD, *that he might be glorified.*" (Isaiah 61: 1–3).

Yes, this was a prophecy of the coming Messiah, given several hundred years before His birth. However, when you read verse six, you will realize that this prophecy is also for you and me personally for we are all to walk in the footsteps of Jesus. ("As He is, so are we in the earth!" 1 John 4:17). Isaiah 61 tells you that you will be healed of whatever mental and spiritual wounds you experience, healed so that you can also minister healing to others. You will be a "walking Bible," an ambassador of the dear Lord Jesus who endured His lonely, earthly walk so that we may be enabled to experience His victorious life and in that process glorify Him.

Will you always remember Him and His promises? Cynthia's testimony demonstrates human frailty: "I wish that I could say that I have always remembered to apply the lessons from that episode in my life to other times when I allowed my thoughts to make me unhappy but I have had to learn over and over again that God wants to give me the mind of Christ and that I must surrender my thoughts to Him before He can bring about that miracle. I praise Him for His long-suffering and patience."

Cynthia's testimony is meant to encourage you to begin a new way of thinking as well. To help you with this new beginning walk, make several photocopies of the chart following this chapter, and use it as long as you need to establish new, positive habit patterns, even those promises concerning the terrible wounds of the past. This may be all you need to begin a beautiful, life-long walk with Jesus, resting in His faithfulness with trust and confidence. *Eternal life does begin on this earth.* What kind of life is this? The word "eternal," according to a Greek Lexicon means, "constant, abiding." Christ is promising you His own constant, abiding life—eternal life—beginning now! How? He promises His life, all of Himself, on His terms with His promises hidden in your heart—with peace from Jesus to shed emotional pain and despair.

YOUR PERSONAL SPIRITUAL WORK PLAN FOR THE DAYS AHEAD

I do not know your prior progress in the Christian walk, but you do and so does Jesus. At this moment, you have begun, or launched further into the process of the regeneration and restoration of your mind and your soul by His Holy Spirit. That Spirit will bring the mind, attitudes and thoughts of Jesus to you often and imbed them into your life.

You are also placing yourself where God can work out His salvation in you by His New Covenant promise to write His law on your mind and heart— His divine nature lived out in you! He will be giving you His own obedient, connected-to-the-Father nature, His own righteousness replacing your carnal heart with the fullness of Himself, which is the most precious answer to all your needs. It may take a little while for you to grasp exactly what that means to you—that the Father is not an "angry God" except to the wicked. To you, He is a tender, merciful Parent, full of compassion for your weary frame. As you understand this, you will be enabled to receive Him every moment. You will meet each new attack of the enemy with joy, for in Him you will find greater fellowship than you ever believed possible.

To begin this priceless new life, spend time in the following activities:

First, use the texts above in the worksheet that follow this lesson, called **A Daily Log**—duplicating extra pages so you will have plenty of space. Rather than charting your feelings with constant introspection throughout the day, when using a strictly Biblical approach it is more effective to often turn to the Word of God and immerse yourself in the Father and His promises, experiencing that close fellowship with Him. When you take His Word, and accept it as coming directly from Himself to you for your present need, *you are becoming what He promised.*

Second, praise God for as many of your blessings as you can think of during the day. Go for walks and recount all the things that the Father as done for you in years past and at the present time.

Third, make a list of people you know who are shut-in and in need of friendship. If you cannot get out to visit, call someone on the phone. Do not discuss yourself and your disappointments or problems. Instead, share something of how God is leading you and developing new hope in your own life. Express your concern for the person, ask if they have any particular needs where you can help, and offer a short prayer for them. If you cannot afford to phone them because of long distance charges, send a letter or an email.

Persist in this program for a week or more then proceed to Lesson two.

TO EXPERIENCE FULL SURRENDER

Ask not for continual mirth and laughter—
but for joy in Jesus through every sorrow.
Ask not for the wind to be always at your back—
but for a wide coat to share with a fellow pilgrim.
Ask not for level ground on which to make your pilgrimage—
but for strength to climb the highest mountains
Ask not for a mansion on earth—
but for the unquenchable desire to lead others to heavenly
mansions.
Ask not for personal happiness—
but rather to bring happiness to others.
Ask not to avoid all lonely hours—
but to experience there the deepest level of fellowship with
Jesus.
Ask not for temporal wants—
but to be emptied of the corroding power of selfishness.
Ask not that you will never meet the enemy—
but that you will recognize him and his tactics.
Ask not to avoid all battles with that enemy—
but to be covered that moment with the full armor of God.
Ask not for continual sunny skies—
but for His protection in the "secret place of the Most
High."
Ask not for constant serenity and peace—
but only to be kept in the eye of the hurricane.

—E. D.

DO YOU REALLY KNOW WHO YOU ARE?

Consider these thoughts each morning—

- that if you feel worthless with no reason for living on this earth...you are permanently "graven on the palms" of His hands. **Isaiah 49:16** Ask Him to show you those nailprints; they spell your name!
- that if you feel "poor in your spirit," in your very inner being, He can now bless you abundantly, opening even the very kingdom of heaven to you...you are now able to receive. Just ask Him! **Matthew 5:3**
- that if you aren't sure of who you are to the King of the Universe, it may be that you have not yet really "tasted" enough to realize that "the Lord is gracious," but by faith you can know that you are "chosen of God and precious." **Psalms 34:8; 1 Peter 2:4**
- That if anyone today touches your life in a negative way, he has "touched the apple of God's eye." **Zechariah 2:8** ...you are that special to Him!
- that if you feel like a pauper, it is the delusion of the enemy, for He has already "made us kings" **Revelation 1:6** to reign first on this earth with victory over that enemy who loves to blind the eyes of his victims. This blindness can be cured with eyesalve that will enable you to see Him in all His glorious character and live to emulate Him. **Revelation 3: 18**
- that if you don't feel very special to anyone, realize that you are one betrothed to King Jesus five ways. What earthly potential bridegroom would give such a present of the best of his own attributes to his would-be bride of righteousness, judgment (or justice), loving-kindness, mercies, and faithfulness? **Hosea 2:19, 20**
- that if you feel dry and spiritless, you may be one refreshed when speaking for God, as you study His precious letter to you His children—the Word of God. **Isaiah 28:9–13**
- that if you doubt that your character matters to anyone, He has called you to be one in whom God's glory is revealed—His very own character. **1 Peter 4:12, 13;**

- that if you have nothing to give to others, you are called to be one who bears fruit as the result of chastening. **Hebrews 5: 10, 11**
- that if you feel you have so little faith, He has called you to be faithful—*through His faithfulness*? What a privilege to accept His mind as your own, and to be *saved by His life*. **Revelation 17:14; Romans 5:10**

Take a moment to thank Him and to praise Him that you are graven on His hands, poor in spirit, chosen of God and precious, the apple of God's eye.

DAILY LOG

Rejoice, for you can experience life—
and that more abundantly—by His promises!

Wrong Thought to be Extinguished with Date	New Thought Pattern Practiced	Scripture Claimed

DAILY LOG—(EXAMPLE)

Rejoice, for you can experience life—
and that more abundantly—by His promises!

Wrong Thought to be Extinguished with Date	New Thought Pattern Practiced	Scripture Claimed
*I say more than I need to say to people...*April 16	God will help me by giving me His Holy Spirit.	"Not by might, not by power, but by My Spirit, saith the Lord."—Zech. 10:12
My life is worthless and I am no good to anyone. April 21	I am worthwhile to God as long as I remain in His will.	"...Thou art my servant; I have chosen thee, and not cast thee away. Fear thou not; for I am with thee; be not dismayed; for I am thy God: I will strengthen thee; yea, I will help thee; yea, I will uphold thee with the right hand of my righteousness."—Isa. 41: 9, 10
I don't think God cares anymore if I do right or wrong. April 23	God is delighted when I choose to love and follow him.	"The LORD thy God in the midst of thee is mighty; he will save, he will rejoice over thee with joy; he will rest in his love, he will joy over thee with singing."—Zeph. 3:17

Lesson 2

RETRAINING YOUR THOUGHT LIFE

TO SAFEGUARD YOUR IMAGINATION

Sally Fields is an attractive actress who was asked to play the part of Sybil, a tormented, so-called, multiple-personality individual. She watched what others had done for similar movies and considered it all as bad acting. She felt she must do more than this to truly portray the lady who lived such a troubled life. She described her decision in these words:

> I sort of had to invent something on my own, sort of go mad myself, just get so emotionally hyped and so exhausted...We worked long hours and it was very, very intense.

There's more; notice this question from the interviewer:

Question: How long did it take to shake Sybil (the multiple personality she was portraying) from your system?
Field: I don't think I ever did. Doing that kind of work is like being hypnotized. The feelings you've portrayed don't go away, because it's really not just acting. You went through this thing; it is real. You can let it go and you can go home, but it's still an experience you had. (*Reader's Digest*, May 2001)

You are wondering now, I suppose, why I am telling you a story of an actress and how playing a part affected her. It's because the story does not end there. An article in the April–May 2006 issue of ***Scientific American Mind*** magazine, tells about recent significant experiments involving MRI observations. MRI stands for Magnetic Resonate Imaging—the wonderful non-invasive way to see what parts of the brain are active during certain activities. Researchers are able to see certain portions of the brain "fire" when they precipitate an action. This enables those researchers to pinpoint where various actions take place in the brain for those locations do not change appreciably from place to place in the brain and neither do those pinpointed spots vary from person to person.

What researchers have found in the brain are groups of "mimicking neurons" firing when a person does a specific action. That part is not so surprising, but what surprised those researchers was to discover that *even when the individual is no longer doing the acting*, but is merely watching someone else doing an action or even reading about it, the mimicking neurons fire *as if they were doing the action themselves*. Suddenly, television viewing and reading material takes on a very different dimension beyond "recreation." The viewer becomes a doer, a participant, along with the actor or actress, in whatever actions are being portrayed—living the life, involved in the doing of whatever is being represented. The viewer is then becoming what he beholds and a certain spiritual reminder can never again be doubted. What is that law? Simply that we become what we behold!

> A long preparatory process, unknown to the world, goes on in the heart before the Christian commits open sin. The mind does not come down at once from purity and holiness to depravity, corruption, and crime. It takes time to degrade those formed in the image of God to the brutal or the satanic. *By beholding, we become changed.* By the indulgence of impure thoughts, man can so educate his mind that sin which he once loathed will become pleasant to him.—***Messages to Young People***, page 282.

What we have been asked to believe by blind faith, is no longer a faith issue, for we can see it by sight-literally! Surely we would want to ignite the right mimicking neurons...

That quote above is more than a nice idea; it's a Biblical truth, as well.

2 Corinthians 3:18—But **we** all, with open face beholding as in a glass the glory of the Lord, are changed into the same image from glory to glory, even as by the Spirit of the Lord.

Of course, God knew this all along. He is the One who put those mirror neurons in our marvelous minds. He knew they were needed for babies to learn to walk and talk, to and use their bodies for all kinds of maneuvers from riding a bike, to

RETRAINING YOUR THOUGHT LIFE • 19

playing ball and climbing trees. He knew we would need this skill even in adulthood to learn new skills and new trades.

God also knew that we would need mirror neurons to look by faith to behold what He is like. We are even told how this can happen, for God has given a promise in His Word;

"Thine eyes shall see the King in His beauty." **Isaiah 33:17**

Is this simply a "someday" promise, a beautiful sentence to remind us that Jesus is coming again to remove us from this wicked planet?

It *is* a "someday" promise, yes, but is it possible that we can also see the beauties of the King today? If we believe that only radiant streams of light fulfill the description of bright streams of glory, we will miss something that God wants us to see and experience now—during these last end-time moments.

Consider this: Which beauties of our King have you "seen" and experienced?

- His great forgiveness: "Father, forgive me, for I did not understand what I was doing." **(Luke 23:34)**
- The Father, running to greet you while you are yet a "great way off." **(Luke 15:20)**
- Felt the drawing of His mercy and His lovingkindness. **(Jeremiah 31:3)**
- The Father singing when you make the right choice to not only believe that He exists, but also to trust Him with your life. **(Zephaniah 3:17)**
- Submitting yourself totally to the Father, even though you may feel laid in the dust. **(John 3:3)**

The above 5 events describe the process of the new birth principle. If you have experienced the New Birth some time in the past, or if you responded positively to the assignments at the end of Lesson 1, this is likely a reality to you. This principle is one of the laws of the universe that guarantees your future happiness and experience with God—on earth—and later as an inhabitant of heaven. If your imagination has not yet attempted to see these unseen realities, you are now invited to begin to train your feeble thinking abilities to see them, to realize that you are approaching the Father and that He is right now running to meet you while you are a long way off. What a blessing when you forsake all your frailties and failures of life and allow the Father to throw His robe around you! What healing of those wounds of the present and past He will bring as you receive Him fully!

Now, how can you make this transition from earthly, carnal living, to a joyful, "in Christ" continuing life experience? Is there a Scripture that promises safety even in the end times that directly precedes the second coming of Jesus?

"He shall dwell on high: his place of defense shall be the munitions of rocks: bread shall be given him; his waters shall be sure." **(Isaiah 33:16).**

The verse directly preceding verse 16, identifies God's blinders and His ear plugs:

"He that walketh righteously, and speaketh uprightly; he that despiseth the gain of oppressions, that shaketh his hands from holding of bribes, that *stoppeth his ears from hearing of blood, and shutteth his eyes from seeing evil*; **(Isaiah 33:15).**

Have you stopped your ears and eyes from hearing and seeing evil? Have you determined to set no wicked thing before you? **(Psalms 101:3).** What are the wicked things in our world today?

"Wicked Thing" List We Must Deal With Constantly

- What we watch on television
- What we read in books
- What magazines we read
- Certain portions of the newspaper we read
- Foolish talk by others around us

The story at the beginning of this chapter is just part of the reason why television viewing or mystery–story reading, for example, is something we must deal with if we don't want "mirror image" neurons turning us into those ugly and sometimes vulgar pictures we see or read about.

Is there anything besides the negative effects of mirror image neurons as reasons for letting go of so much of what the world around us has to offer as tasty morsels?

Plenty of reasons! If you've been protected all your lives from horrible, devastating experiences from brutal attacks on your fellowmen, for example, then should something like this happen before your eyes, you would be filled with fear and horror. You would experience acute compassion and sympathy for the pain inflicted on the individual. However, if you have watched countless attacks of senseless brutality on television or videos (even true portrayals of historical brutality during wartime concentration camps, for example) you could not help those people portrayed, and you would have been in the process of being numbed to such acts. Your mind has been effectively taught to be disassociated from a person being stalked on a dark street, and to do nothing to help. You will have been numbed to the pain of other people and what they are experiencing. You will be unable to fulfill a Bible principle that says,

"Bear ye one another's burdens, and so fulfill the law of Christ." (**Galatians 6:2**).

Common scenes of terror and fear cause the brain to form a kind of self-protectiveness that makes a person lose compassion for humanity. That care for humanity is the very reason we are on the earth. Even as the Messiah came to "fulfill the law," He places us here to allow Him to again fulfill that law by being His hands and feet.

So those "evil imaginations" feeders need to be "cast down," (**2 Corinthians 10:5**), but if that's all you did, your mind would be left a hollow box! God asks you to *let Him* direct your imagination! He can only do this if you turn your face from the ugly, the vile, and the impure to His beauties— His marvelous creation. One important verse provides the keys to determining the focus and interest of our minds.

Philippians 4:8—"Finally, brethren, whatsoever things are true, whatsoever things are honest, whatsoever things are just, whatsoever things are pure, whatsoever things are lovely, whatsoever things are of good report; if there be any virtue, and if there be any praise, think on these things."

What were those thought inhabitors? True, honest, just, pure, lovely, good report, virtue and praise.

How can we work in harmony with God to retrain our minds?

Only God knows what is really in our hearts. "I the Lord search the heart, I try the reins (inner-most thoughts)" (**Jeremiah 17:10**).

If you have only lately become a Christian, or if you are yearning at this moment to begin that process, you realize that most of your imaginations right now are based on those "pictures of the world" and its evils. You must be patient with yourself for they were not put in there in a moment, and neither will they be erased in a few moments.

As you set your mind to view only the good, the pure, and the lovely, you are allowing Him from now on to redirect your imagination, because He knows what is really in your heart. He also knows that you need to know what He is like and what He is able to do in you and for you.

You can see the contrast between His thoughts and your thoughts when you read His Word. Moreover you are training your imagination *to think His thoughts* when you read...

- the **Gospel of John** where we see with mind's eye, the gentle, caring life of Jesus
- how Joseph stood firm during times of temptation in Egypt **(Genesis 39).**
- how Abraham chose to obey God when God asked him to kill his son. **(Genesis 22).**
- of Jacob wrestling with an angel, clinging in faith until he was blessed. **(Genesis 32).**
- of David who was not afraid of a lion, a bear or a heathen giant. **(2 Samuel 21).**
- of Daniel & friends who purposed in their hearts not to defile themselves.**(Daniel 1).**
- of these same 3 friends who chose to obey God and not a heathen King. **(Daniel 3).**

Assignment 1: Read the book of John over the next few days in your devotional time, and then these familiar Bible stories, even if you have read them before, and ask God to reveal the depth of the love demonstrated by these giants of faith recorded in Scripture. You will realize how much they were like us even though they lived thousands of years ago.

We can see that *the thinking* of these heroes of faith in Bible times was followed by firm actions for right. They illustrate the truth that their imaginations were fed the truth of God first, causing a firm determination to do the right thing, no matter what the result might be. They show us that when we—

1) know the right principles, we can more easily
2) allow God to control our thoughts, thoughts that are then
3) followed by our feelings and these altogether make up the person.

Here is a most-important law of your being: *your thoughts and your feelings make up your character—their sum total equals you!*

"For as he thinketh in his heart, so is he." (**Proverbs 23:7**).

You are allowing God to begin the process of building and fashioning you into a person of steadfast integrity, bound intimately to the Father in a close, loving relationship.

Not only will you experience all of the above, but you will be in the every-moment sealing process of settling your own mind that He is yours and you are His, not for a little while, but for eternity. That means that at every moment that you must make a decision it will be made with this thought in mind, "If I make this choice, will it be part of the process of drawing me closer into an intimate relationship with the Father and the Son, or will it make a wider chasm between my soul and His soul?"

If the choice is still a struggle, ask God to give you a mental picture of the relationship between you and this King of the universe. As you have read of the many indications of how He wants a close fellowship with you, are you finding yourself snuggling closer to Him? Yes? Question yourself, "Then do I really want to spoil that oneness, that close bonding, by questioning how He is leading in my life, even being angry with Him, or by ignoring Him?"

If the answer is "no," are their still barriers to such a relationship? There may still be hidden unresolved pain, perhaps resentment and bitterness. In the next chapter we will address the way to bring healing of those deeper disappointments of life.

Here is the continuing promise from Isaiah 33:

"Thine eyes shall see the king in his beauty: they shall behold the land that is very far off." (**Isaiah 33:16, 17**).

Yes, someday soon our eyes will really see the King in His beauty, radiant with real beams of glory, and with a crown on His head, coming with clouds of angels to receive those who have been thinking of Him, contemplating Him, desiring Him, those who have been experiencing being intimately bound fast to Him.

But don't miss this: We can see Him also by faith today—the beauty of His character of much more value than the trash of television, the smut of novels, or the intrigue of the lives of Hollywood idols. We can see the land that is very far off—by faith—real faith that goes beyond believing.

"But as many *as received Him,* to them gave he power to become the sons of God, even to them *that believe on His name.*" **John 1:12**

This verse contains two important words—"received" and "believe." You see it takes more than believing there is a God; it takes even more than believing that He is the Creator. It is not enough to know that He died for the sins of everyone in the world. It matters most that you view Him as your personal Savior—a fact that enables you to submit to Him totally and receive His power to become a child of God, for confident trust in him brings *His faithfulness* to your soul. In short form, belief + trust = faith.—and it's all of Him, through Him, and because of Him. Whatever amount of faith we can muster up is only good enough to allow His faithfulness to work in you!

You will value it, desire it, and more than that—be *continually desiring Him,* for your mind will have been retrained to think of and appreciate Him and His purity. You will not be satisfied every morning with less than a renewed, born-again experience. You will follow Him wherever He goes in "abiding fellowship with cleaving trust!" (Which is a Lexicon rendition of the meaning of the word "follow.") (See Revelation 14:4).

CONTINUING TO RETRAIN YOUR THOUGHT LIFE

Outlined below are more suggestions for continuing to build strong confidence in God, so that you will be trained to think in new, positive, and ever-developing ways of His direction to meet your own situations and troubles. Determine to face each new day of darkness or pain with hope and assurance that God loves you and means to draw you to Him. Fill your mind with thoughts of the Father and His desires for you. Look at the following thought-building list as a prescription, and as the way to develop a closer relationship with the Father and His Son. Allow His Spirit to work His healing, transforming work of grace and glory in your life—grace that provided you with reconciliation to the Father from your past by His death, *and power to live His glorious character by His life infused in you as you submit to Him.* (See Romans 5:10).

Continue any meaningful suggestions from Lesson One. Use the following first three steps each day, for a week.

1. Even if you feel your trust and confidence is small, *tell God that you trust Him.*

2. Ask your heavenly Father to *show you where you lack confidence in Him.* Continue reading your Bible each day, and watch for His answers to come from His Book, through the ministry of time spent in His created works, and through events that you know could only have been orchestrated by Him. Ask God to bind you to Him in love, listening for His voice in the messages of the Word.

During the second week and for several weeks following, add any of the following activities to numbers one and two;

3. Read the Bible Study, and the words of the song, Sealed For Eternity, and rejoice that you have received all of Jesus and that you are in the healing, sealing process.

4. Notice those texts that are promises—opening up fresh ways of experiencing more of Jesus in His fullness. *Memorize and thank Him for them as problems arise.*

5. Find 10 new things every day for which you are grateful. *Praise and thank the Creator for His provisions.* As often as possible, do this while walking or resting in the sunshine.

6. Learn several old hymns of faith. Sing them while you work—sing them in your heart when you cannot sing them aloud. Pay no attention to your feelings; give the Father an "offering of praise," the kind of sacrifice He wants today. Isn't it a sacrifice to let go of the way you feel justified in feeling—sad, morose and even angry? The old you would pity yourself—now He asks that you offer praise instead, showing confidence in God. As you say *"Father, I love You and I trust You, no matter what!" and sing or listen to recordings of hymns, submitting your life in trust to your heavenly Father,* you will experience the miracle of His joy in your heart.

(Remember, if your mind wanders into negative thoughts, rehearsing the unkind actions of others, or if you feel sorry or angry about old or new events, talk confidence in God aloud, saying "Father, I love You and I trust You, no matter what!" Quote a promise you have learned and *tell Him you believe He is doing it*! Never mind how you feel about it or how impossible it appears.)

Finally, remember this important principle:

7. When someone asks how you are doing, give no negative recital of your trials. Answer with assurance that your heavenly Father is your best Friend, or that you are thankful for His love—any comment that gives Him glory. *These responses will react back on your own mind, building your own faith and confidence and allowing Him to work His work in you.* Remember: every event that seems to be a troubling situation to face is a chance to learn and build a trusting relationship with God.

SEALED FOR ETERNITY
Supplement to Lesson 2
A Song of Experience for God's People at the End of Time
Inspired by Song of Solomon 8:6

Borne on His heart long before my birth, **(Isaiah 44: 1, 2)**
Named as His own for He knew my worth, **(Isaiah 43:1)**
Carved on His hands when He died for me; **(Isaiah 49:16)**
Purchased at Calvary. **(John 3:16)**
Sealed on His mighty arm of power; **(Song of Solomon 8:6)**
Sealed on His great heart of love, **(Song of Solomon 8:6)**
Ransomed from sin at Calvary; **(II Corinthians 1:10)**
Loved from eternity **(Jeremiah 31:3)**

Sought many days with repentant tears, **(Acts 3:19)**
Yielded at last as He took my fears, **(2 Timothy 1:7)**
Glory and praise to Christ my King, **(Psalms 47: 6, 7)**
Praise through eternity. **(Revelation 19: 5, 6)**
Sealed—I'll be sealed in heart and mind, **(Revelation 7:3)**
Living to serve and obey. **(Daniel 7:27)**
Bound to His heart with selfless love; **(Hosea 11:4)**
Sealed for eternity **(Revelation 22: 10, 11)** E. D.

Lesson 3

ESCAPE FROM BITTERNESS

FINDING ESCAPE TOOLS THAT WORK

My way home from school meant walking a board sidewalk along a very quiet street. Since this street was really a road that hugged Mt. Nebo in our hometown, this sidewalk on only one side of this street provided my total choice for how I would walk home. I dreaded it because here I was off the school grounds and "fair game" to Johnny—the terror of my life.

Why he continually harassed and tortured me at every turn, I never knew. This day would be only another episode in a long list of meanness from his hand. Sure enough, a glance behind me revealed that the running feet on the old board sidewalk belonged to Johnny and he was coming fast. But what could he do to me at that speed?

My shock turned to agonizing pain as his incredibly well-timed jump to grasp the over-handing tree limb brought it down squarely on the middle of my head. No, I didn't faint; I reeled with pain and saw a few stars, but my firmly-knit skull bones held firm while Johnny's loud and wicked laughter wafted back to me as he raced on down the hill. Sometimes for years afterward I would imagine I could still feel that pain on my head!

No, I lost no love on Johnny and certainly would have never named a son of mine by that name. Neither would I name one of them "Teddy," and would have cringed if any son of mine should carry that carrot red hair of my other mean tormentor of school days. Years would go by before I learned about how my bitterness-poor-me attitude was blocking victory in other areas of my life.

You or someone you know may be thinking at this point, "Well, those childhood skirmishes don't hold a candle to what I've experienced. What if *my* dark valley is the result of really terrible wrongs done to me, or unethical and perhaps shameful actions of a significant person in my life. I think I have good reason to respond with angry or bitter feelings and words."

I do know about that as well—far beyond children's pranks. I had to discover one precious key to resolving bitterness many years later when someone phoned me with some very unsavory piece of information I needed, but that made me heartsick and broken again. My first response was to run to my bedroom, fall to my knees and sob out my despair to the Father. This was an earlier incident in a string of events that happened some years before being pulled over by the highway patrolman.

It didn't take long to realize that I was repeating a pattern given up months before, a surrender that brought about huge changes in my attitudes, demeanor and living in Christ. Remembering this, I dried my eyes, stood up, and walked to the piano. Determined to continue the earlier resolution to remain in a surrendered state to the Father, I put my fingers on the keys. I did not feel like playing and certainly not like singing. I could only think, "My Father loves me as much today as He loved me yesterday before I knew any of this!" I began to play, not an old hymn, not one of the personal compositions the Father had already given me, but a simple new chorus of confidence and trust. From my fingers and from my mouth the melody and the words came together—straight from the throne of God—"Because He loves me, my heart is glad; Because He loves me, I can't be sad. With joy or' flowing my being fills, with love enfolding, my glad heart thrills!"

Surprised by wonder and joy, I sang it again and yet again, afraid to stop for fear I would lose it. The sadness of ten minutes earlier had been pushed aside and replaced miraculously with the solid blessedness of peace in Jesus. That day will never fade from my mind—not because of the hurt I received from another soul, but because of what Jesus did in my moment of despair when I surrendered it all to Him!

Yes, it is easy for the human heart to see the unfairness, the thoughtlessness, or even the absolute meanness of another individual who should be a significant person to us—whether parent, spouse, child, or close friend. Dealing with all that unfairness and cruelty is not easy. This is why these lessons contain this one whole chapter alone with the focus on resolving bitterness. Bitterness is not the only contributor to a depressive, sorrowful state of despair, but since it is such a large factor, we want to suggest some ways of dealing with this *root* that will bring significant results. In the Bible, "root" is synonymous with "heart," so we can also say that bitterness is likely the heart of many other problems.

Check *in your mind*, any of the following statements you see as true about yourself. This is your *personal inventory* and need not be viewed by others, whether friends or counselor. The *"Wonderful Counselor" (Jesus)* has answers for you—samples on the next page.

Childhood Disappointments:
1. I was unfairly treated as a child
2. I was often left out of activities
3. I was molested as a child
4. I received no real care from one or both parents when I was growing up

If you agreed mentally with even one of these 4 possible childhood disappointments above, you likely have many of the following views of yourself.

pathetic shamed trashed ugly violated vulnerable dirty

What About Adult Disappointments? Mentally check this list:
5. I feel sorry for myself when I miss out on what someone else gets.
6. I am often lonely
7. I am very hurt over something someone did or said to me, or about me.
8. I feel impatient or even angry while driving in heavy traffic or on the freeway
9. I feel like fighting
10. I feel like even God has let me down.

11. I feel really furious and irate when people do not do as I ask
12. I am resentful and bitter when it seems others take advantage of me

If you mentally checked any of the last 6 feelings above, you may view yourself like some of the descriptions given here in italics.

used outcast useless abandoned degraded empty rejected mistreated misunderstood hated scorned ignored

If you agreed with *any* of the above, I suggest you audibly pray this prayer *to Jesus, the healer of all hurt, the balm for all wounds.*

Ps. 38:22—*"Make haste to help me*, O Lord my salvation."

If Jesus has already ministered His healing to you, or if you did *not* mentally check any of the above descriptions, *Jesus can use you to help other hurting people.* Whether for yourself or others, a negative attitude threatens everyone who has been used and abused.

I know how hopeless it feels at first. *The cure for bitterness* is easy to say but far harder to execute. What is that one-word cure?

Forgiveness! Yes, the carnal heart must often struggle with many of the feelings listed above, but God wants to take every hurting, pain-filled heart, and begin the process of providing the only effective and lasting remedy—*placing His own compassionate, forgiving mind and feelings in you.*

I know; if you could have forgiven your parents, that thoughtless caregiver, that mean, cruel classmate, or that biased, insensitive teacher, you would have done so long before this. The experiences were real; they were cutting and they were cruel. You know the reality of pain that lives today in you as strong as when you first experienced it. You may feel no ability or inclination—certainly no power to forgive such meanness.

But Jesus did! Whether those cruel individuals ever know it or not, you may never know, but *Jesus forgave them anyway.* His words on the cross, "Father, forgive them for they know not what they do," revealed the depths of His love for *all mankind, and even reached down to include those insensitive people in your life. Those words included you and me as well!*

That old carnal heart does not have the capacity, the agape love, or the right nature to forgive like Jesus did.

Isaiah 55:7, 8—"Let the wicked forsake his way, and the unrighteous man his thoughts: and let him return unto the LORD, and he will have mercy upon him; and to our God, for he will abundantly pardon. For my thoughts are not your thoughts, neither are your ways my ways, saith the LORD."

Here is the way the Old Testament prophet described God's pardon, His forgiveness, a forgiveness so full, so rich and deep that *it encompassed all the ugliness, all the degraded thinking, and every depraved action of all humanity.* That word, "pardon" in verse 7, is *not* used of the forgiveness of one human to another when simple mistakes wound and hurt but rather of the depth of cruelty addressed in this paragraph.

This kind of deep, heartfelt pardon, this heavenly forgiveness, is only possible with the divine nature of the Godhead— the kind promised in **2 Peter 1:4.**

And there is the secret, the key to your future freedom in Christ. Because you are promised that you may have the "mind that was in Christ Jesus," (**Philippians 2:5**) *you may have His depth of forgiveness.* Because we are promised a "new heart," that heart of agape love is really already yours, complete with full pardon for those who have hurt you in the past. Because you are promised that you can be "partakers of the divine nature," *His forgiving nature has already forgiven your tormenters.* Whether they ever accept His forgiveness and experience it, is up to them, but *the offer and promise is there for you to take and bestow on those who have wounded you.* You must have that healing *whether they are involved or not.* You are only responsible for your own decisions—your own thoughts and feelings—that foundation for who you are becoming.

Submitting to this healing process from the God of the universe may seem utterly impossible to consider. It is humbling to let go of your "right" to remain aloof, angry and bitter against those who have despitefully used you. But do you have any "rights?" Not really—if you have decided to follow the One who gave up heaven for you.

In accepting His mind *and His nature*, you are following the Messiah Who stepped down from His exalted place beside the Father so that you could enjoy eternity with Him forever. *He then writes His law of love, kindness and compassion on your mind.* You receive from the Father a crown today, and you continue to progress in becoming what you never thought you could become, for He has promised...

Psalms 103:4—"Who redeemeth thy life from destruction; *who crowneth thee with lovingkindness and tender mercies;*"

Yes, we are promised a crown of life when Jesus comes, but *today* we may have the crown of Christ's nature, His thoughts and feelings—*even His lovingkindness and tender mercy*. Consider this; if we do not accept His offered life, even His divine nature (**2 Peter 1:4**), we suffer great loss, for *it is the answer to living a righteous life by His faithfullness*. Jesus brought us a warning and testimony through His servant John the Revelator...

Revelation 3:9—"Let no man take thy crown."

Would you allow that thoughtless, unkind individual who caused you so much pain to *also take your crown—the crown you may wear today? Surely not!* If you resist being controlled by anyone, this church sign message puts it in perspective:

"The person who causes you to feel hurt and angry, controls you!"

Instead, you can now be filled with the sensitive, caring, compassionate love of Jesus in your soul.

My prayer for you—"Father, may the one who reads these thoughts at this moment, come in submission right now to receive the precious promised mind of Jesus[1], *whose very life saves us*[2] from **sin**—*our old **carnal nature**. Fill this individual

with Your forgiveness proffered at the cross in the prayer of Jesus, 'Father, forgive them for they know not what they do.'(3) In the wonderful name of our Savior, Jesus Christ, Amen."
(1) Philippinas 2:5 (2) Romans 5:10 (3) Luke 23:24

This is the time to begin learning more of God's promises to counter the old hurts of the past, and allow Christ to bind up your wounds, heal your pain and bring hope and healing to your life. Consider the following texts. Numbers of promises match with the same number of painful areas listed in the first part of this lesson.

1 **Unfairly treated as a child:** "For we have not an high priest which cannot be touched with the feeling of our infirmities; but was in all points tempted like as we are, yet without sin. Verse 16: Let us therefore come boldly unto the throne of grace that **we may obtain mercy**, and find grace to help in time of need." (**Hebrews 4:15, 16**).

2. **Often left out of activities:** "That we *henceforth be no more children*, tossed to and fro, and carried about with every wind of doctrine, by *the sleight of men*, and cunning craftiness, whereby they lie in wait to deceive; But speaking the truth in love, *may grow up into him in all things*, which is the head, even Christ:" (**Ephesians 4:14, 15**).

3. **Molested as a child.** "So that contrariwise ye ought **rather to forgive him, and comfort him**, lest perhaps such a one should be swallowed up with overmuch sorrow." (**2 Corinthians 2:7**).

4. **Received no real care from one or both parents.** "**Forgive and ye shall be forgiven.**" (**Luke 6:37**

5. **Feel sorry for myself when missing out on what someone else gets.** "Casting all your care upon him; for **he careth for you.**" (**1 Peter 5:7**).

6. **Often lonely.** "But my God shall supply all your need according to his riches in glory by Christ Jesus." (**Philippians 4:19**).

7. **Hurt over something someone did or said to me or about me.** "**Not rendering evil for evil, or railing for railing**: but **contrariwise blessing;** knowing that ye are thereunto called, that ye should inherit a blessing." (**1 Peter 3:9**).

8. **Feel angry when driving in heavy traffic or on the freeway.** "For we wrestle not against flesh and blood, **but against principalities, against powers, against the rulers of the darkness of this world, against spiritual wickedness in high places. Wherefore take unto you the whole armor of God,** that ye may be able to withstand in the evil day, and *having done all, to stand.*" **(Ephesians 6:12, 13).** The answer to number 7 works here as well! Road rage can be cured by thinking of the other driver as someone who needs a blessing. Their thoughtless action of cutting in front of you, then slowing down might not even be noticed if they are thinking hard and trying to solve a personal problem. They might need your blessing not your angry thoughts. Even if it seems so apparent that they were purposefully rude, it is all the more reason to pray that they will somehow be blessed. God will hear that kind of prayer.

9. **Feel like fighting.** "But of him are ye in *Christ Jesus, who of God is made unto us wisdom, and righteousness, and sanctification, and redemption:*" **(1 Corinthians 1:30).** Have you noticed this promise of how Jesus was made to be all these things for you? The burden is all on Him. Let Him carry you.

10. **Feeling like even God has let me down.** "*Go ye therefore, and teach all nations,* baptizing them in the name of the Father, and of the Son, and of the Holy Ghost: Teaching them to observe all things whatsoever I have commanded you: and, lo, *I am with you alway, even unto the end of the world.*" **(Matthew 28:20).**

11. **Feeling really furious and irate.** "**Be ye angry and sin not.**" **(Ephesians 4:22).** It's alright to be angry, but be sure you know who deserves the reflection of that anger. God identifies them in Psalms; they are not your friends, relatives or significant people; they are Satan and his helpers. The demonic forces have ganged up on that one who is annoying you; he or she is a captive to the will of the real enemy. This is the time that this individual needs your compassion, not your criticism or censure. This is the time for you to fall on your knees before the Father and plead for His mercy for this person and for you to claim the wisdom He has promised in

James 1:5—"If any of you lack wisdom, let Him ask of God who giveth to all men liberally."

12. **Feeling resentful and bitter at my lot in life**. "Looking diligently lest any man fail of the grace of God; lest any root of bitterness springing up trouble you and thereby many be defiled." (Hebrews 12:15). God is offering to take your root of bitterness; He will take care of it for you. *Your job is to give up that bitter root, to take Jesus, the "root out of a dry ground."* **(Isaiah 53:2).**

Some emotions are tough to handle for they tend to eat at our very inner core nature. How can you possibly find that forgiveness to minister in certain wrenching circumstances of life? You may read it and see if you don't agree that it holds the key.

Penny came to a church as a visitor seeking answers. As a non-church attendee, she felt she was really going out on a limb, but she was desperate enough to do anything. Fortunately the pastor noticed and read her face and spoke to her briefly before she left, promising to come with his wife to see her in the afternoon. During the conversation in her home, he led her to Christ, helping her in a prayer of thanksgiving and dedication with specific Bible promises.

Then she wanted to quit smoking so the pastor showed her films of diseased lungs, gave medical facts of the harmfulness of smoking and guided her in how to drink more liquids and other helpful hints to quit the habit but there was no success. She next attended a regular Stop Smoking clinic hosted by the church, then an evangelistic series. Penny continued her struggle over cigarettes while the pastor and his wife prayed. Occasionally he asked her how she was doing which she and he both translated to mean, "Have you had victory yet over cigarettes?" One day he was impressed *not* to ask that question for it could only be embarrassing for her to have to say, "no." As quickly as he was impressed not to ask that question and wondering what he should say instead, the Lord impressed him with these words, "Penny, I want you to stop trying to quit smoking!"

The comment surprised the pastor as much as it surprised Penny. He did not have to wonder long what she should be encouraged to do instead of struggling against cigarettes. The Lord led in the next words from the pastor's mouth.

"Penny, do you still believe those texts that we read the day you accepted Jesus as your Lord and Savior?"

"Oh, yes!" she assured him.

"Then I want you to thank Him for His gift of salvation, and how much you appreciate what He is doing in your life. Praise Him for the Bible promises you accepted that day when you accepted Jesus as your personal Savior. Even if you put a cigarette to your lips and take a drag, thank the Lord for His precious gift of salvation. He will bless you."

Penny agreed and the pastor left. He saw her several nights at the meetings that continued at the church, but she volunteered no information and he continued the pact with God and himself not to ask. One evening he noticed that she stood outside the church for a little while after shaking hands at the door. She was talking to another lady who was known to also be battling with the smoking habit. He was delighted to hear Penny say to the other individual, "Don't try to stop smoking because it doesn't work! Just thank the Lord for His wonderful salvation. I've been doing that for a week and I haven't smoked once and I don't believe I ever will!"

And she never did!

If praising God and thanking Him for what He has already done for us on a physical level, works so dramatically, can we trust Him any less with our spiritual, emotional and mental health? We do not need to question it; He will. It's called trusting Him to finish the good work in us that He has already started.

> But when we really believe that God loves us and means to do us good, we shall cease to worry about the future. We shall trust God as a child trusts a loving parent. Then our troubles and torments will disappear, for our will is swallowed up in the will of God.—**Mount of Blessing 100, 101 (1896).**

To Think About:

1. If this all seems too big for you to grasp at this moment, what can you do? Give God time to work in your life. Continue the assignments at the end of Lesson One and Two that are the most meaningful to you. Thank God that He is lifting you above any pain you may be harboring from present or past unjust actions of others.

2. *Are you rejoicing in the forgiveness of God, and the cleansing of your own soul that you have needed for so long? Are you beginning to experience victories as you claim these promises from God's Word?* If this is so, you are experiencing a little of the showers of the Early Rain of God's Spirit promised in His Word, as real as spring showers in April.

3. Study the **Wounded for Grafting** Bible study and thank God that you are receiving His very life blood shed for you at the cross—the "sap," as it were, running from His veins to yours. Praise Him for this "blood transfusion" of His life.

SUFFICIENCY IN HIM

I asked to see Your face—The blessing of your smile;
Instead, You held me close in thought awhile.
I asked to feel You clasp my hand with gentle touch,
Instead Your Word revealed You love me—Oh, so much!

I asked to feel Your arm across my shoulder,
Instead You made me strong for you—and bolder!
I asked to see Your footprints in the sands of time,
But I found more; Your prints were deeply meshed in mine

I asked to feel no more the wrath of Satan's ire, (Revelation 12:12)
You chose instead to cleanse my life with heav'nly fire. (Daniel 7:10)
And all the while You burned each briar and ev'ry thorn, (Isaiah 27:3, 4)
Your Spirit washed my heart till Christ in me was born. (Revelation 12:12)

CHORUS:
Now I find sufficiency in Him,
As He gives, I take His promised mind,
When through Him I triumph over sin;

He will suffice and bind my heart to Him.
Yes, I have struggled, I have cried, But praise Him!
He traded His perfection for my pride. E. D.

WOUNDED FOR GRAFTING

John 15:5—*"I am the vine, ye are the branches:* He that abideth in me, and I in him, the same bringeth forth much fruit: for without me ye can do nothing.

We have known for a very long time that *He is the vine* and *we are but branches.* But how did we come to be branches, for did not we come from wild stock? Not until we recognized this lovely vine did we desire to be part of it. One day we learned the truth: He had already made provision for us to be grafted in.

Romans 11:16, 17—"For if the firstfruit be holy, the lump is also holy: and if the root be holy, so are the branches. And if some of the branches be broken off, and **thou, being a wild olive tree, wert grafted in among them,** and with them partakest of the root and fatness of the olive tree."

He prepared the way for this grafting-in process for **Isaiah 53:5** says, "...**He** was **wounded** for our transgressions."

More than that...

Continuing verse 5: "He was *bruised* for our iniquities..."; "bruised" to prepare for us to be grafted in to Him.

Plant propagators know a wonderful secret that spells success when the graft of a stubborn twig does not easily "take." *The propagator knows what to do; his solution is to "bruise it!"*

I Peter 4: 12, 13—"Beloved, **think it not strange concerning the fiery trial which is to try you,** as though some strange thing happened unto you: But rejoice, **inasmuch as ye are partakers of Christ's sufferings;** that, when his glory shall be revealed, ye may be glad also with exceeding joy."

Yet our heavenly Parent-Stock vine will not bruise without mercy for he knows how much we can take.

Isaiah 42:3—"A *bruised reed shall he not break,* and *the smoking flax shall He not quench*: He shall bring forth judgment unto truth. (**Isaiah 42:3**).

Most precious in this grafting process is how the graft is then cared for. It is not left hanging precariously, but is <u>bound fast with special tape</u>, then covered with plastic. "Strengthen (**Heb.** *chazaq*—**to be bound fast**) the weak hands, confirm the feeble knees." (**Isaiah 35:3**).

"I am the Vine, ye are the branches," Christ said to His disciples. Though He was about to be removed from them, their spiritual union with Him was to be unchanged.

"The connection of the branch with the vine," He said, "represents the relation you are to sustain to Me."

The scion is engrafted into the living vine, and *fiber by fiber, vein by vein, it grows into the vine stock. The life of the vine becomes the life of the branch.* So the soul dead in trespasses and sins receives life through connection with Christ. By faith in Him as a personal Savior the union is formed. The sinner unites his weakness to Christ's strength, his emptiness to Christ's fullness, his frailty to Christ's enduring might. Then he has the mind of Christ. The humanity of Christ has touched our humanity, and our humanity has touched divinity. Thus through the agency of the Holy Spirit man becomes a partaker of the divine nature. He is accepted in the Beloved. (**DA 675.3**)

And as is true in plant grafting so with every child of God; it takes time, not by a one-time rude thrust, or even a wonderful meeting at the foot of the cross, or the washing of baptism.

This beautiful picture of the grafting-in process is for us individually, but also reminds us that the newly baptized person is a "new graft." Our constant prayer should be, what can we do to build this close bonding that strengthens me in Jesus. Also, how can I strengthen other new Christians to help to bind them fast to the Savior in his new position? We can only strengthen others when we are connected ourselves.

Luke 22:32—"But I have prayed for thee, that thy faith fail not: and when thou art converted, strengthen thy brethren."

Isaiah 57:14—"As we live as true Christians, with Christ in us "the hope of glory" (character), only then will we <u>truly</u> "take up the stumbling block out of the way of my people."

We will be ready to "give a reason of the hope that is in us"—God's New Covenant promise that He would write His law on our hearts. (Hebrews 10:16) We know and demonstrate that His promises are real for He has written His law on our hearts; we obey His commands *out of love—moment by moment.* Don't let this all overwhelm you! If there is one paragraph that you can grasp, take it as your own; hang onto it like life itself. If it is a Bible promise, put it on a card and place it in a prominent place in your home. Carry it with you while you walk and meditate on it. Thank God for the promise and rejoice in what He is doing in your life.

It is no fun to be "wounded and bruised!" Our initial response may be shock, dismay or even great sadness, but if we soon remember that this is a "test," a trial to prepare us for grafting in a little deeper to the parent stock, He will turn our sadness to a precious constant, abiding in Him—eternal life in Jesus.

HOLD IT!

Have you begun to wonder, doesn't *anyone else* have responsibilities? Yes, they do have responsibilities! Shouldn't the perpetrator of wrong ever be held accountable? Certainly! Is it best for you to suffer on month after month and year after year without a murmur? No, it is not! Even God's patience and merciful love for mankind will not forever continue to overlook man's rebellion. For now, submit to His precious inner healing no matter what goes on around you. Let God take care of your emotional life as you surrender it all to Him. Trusting Him and managing your mind according to His principles of peace and joy will care for your emotions more than you can imagine.

The truth is, we must deal with ourselves first. The "normal," carnal nature of human beings is to rise up with self-justification. You know the response, "This isn't fair!" "You have no right to act like that, or talk to me that way!" The trouble is, if we only react "normally," we will never solve the problem or inspire our "enemy" to change, or to seek help. That is why it is important for us to exchange our old nature, for His "born again" new nature and through you demonstrate full forgiveness to the sinner. Christ then *stands ready to work through us* to bring the one who wounds us near to Himself.

As you consecrate yourself to Jesus, you are enabled to minister His love to others through you. "Consecrate" literally means, "fill the hand of," and is illustrated by the consecration of Aaron and His sons for the sanctuary service. Even so your hand can be filled with His grace, His mercy and His power today to minister to those around you.

FILL MY HAND

1. *I lift my hands in prayer and supplication;*
And plead my need, the filling of your power;
I give my all in total consecration,
And take to give your love in earth's dark hour.

CHORUS:
Fill my hand, Lord this morning
Fill it now that I may give of your love to others I shall meet
*   today,*
Fill my mind with your Spirit, anoint my feet to walk in your
*   way,*
Bringing joy to every heart

2. *I lift my heart, the spring of thought and action,*
And storm the throne for blessing more and more,
I tarry here in love and adoration Invade my mind
From heaven's bounteous store.

3. *Oh plant my feet, to walk in your salvation,*
To follow paths where saints of old have trod,
Use me to bring your love to every nation
That they may learn to know and serve my God.   E. D.

Lesson 4

WHEN FORGIVENESS SEEMS TOO DIFFICULT—

YOU NEED A HEART

Jason was a four-year-old boy with lots of energy. When his Aunt Rita insisted that he come down from a ladder for his own safety, he became very upset with her. He stomped off in a huff and went away to nurse his angry feelings.

Later, at lunch time, Grandma noticed some smiles returning to Jason's formerly grumpy face.

"You aren't angry at Aunt Rita anymore?" Grandma asked.

"Well, my head still wants to be angry with her, but *my heart keeps changing my mind.*"

Words of wisdom from a little boy, words to bring *healing and glorious, on-going daily victories, when you allow your heart to keep changing your mind!*

It is the new you, who has been born again, and daily chooses to be drawn into an experience and fellowship with God. Old resentments have been resolved, but all is not always well, for now you still find yourself under minor, even severe attacks from a loved one, friend, or church member. You also find yourself extremely disappointed at times to find yourself reacting with old, ingrained habit patterns in one or more of the following ways:

- arguing your point
- defending yourself
- lashing back with similar accusations
- stalking out of the house
- clamming up
- throwing things

However, you realize immediately that those actions are not the way Jesus would react, so you may have tried other tactics to deal with these distressing situations. You might have tried...

- biting your tongue
- counting to ten
- ignoring the individual
- not talking to the person at all, even for several days

or any number of techniques promised to be effective. Even when they seemed to work and you did not reply in an un-Christlike manner, you came away emotionally bruised and bleeding, wondering why this experience had to be, and how this fit into God's plan for your life. When you were "born again," you thought it was the beginning of a new life. You really thought you were now "grown up" into Christ, but wonder how that is possible because your old friends have not changed. Your old troubles with relatives who are thoughtless and unkind stir up emotions that you thought were completely gone.

You know intellectually that you have been forgiven of the past, cleansed and made right with God. *Do you know it with your whole heart?* Do you know it with your feelings—your inner soul? You are recognizing what that main emotion is now however and that recognition is a step. It's that old enemy, "anger."

Don't the psychologists say that harboring anger and not getting it out of your system is damaging to yourself? Yes, they do, and the Christian can agree with that principle. Merely holding your tongue when someone makes you angry is not beneficial to your health—mental or physical!

You remember the antidote for ridding your life of bitterness, don't you? Forgiveness! You also learned that *bitterness is built-up, harbored resentment blown up into anger.* So today when you are confronted again with some of those circumstances that could easily bring you back to a state of bitterness, your present challenge is to forgive your antagonist, and to do so quickly,

Matthew 5:25—"Agree with thine adversary quickly, while thou art in the way with him."

It's the kind thing to do.

But you say you don't *feel* kind; you don't *feel* like agreeing with "your adversary." *Then offer the forgiveness of Jesus, and praise Him for making that possible.*

"Forgiveness is continual kindness toward undeserving individuals."

Read that sentence often. Where have you heard about forgiveness toward undeserving people before? Right! In the story of Jesus and His death on the cross. And only the forgiveness of Jesus that He seasoned with His blood will do. It was for you *and for your antagonist—and neither one of you were deserving of receiving His gift of reconciliation with the Father.*

Remember that we already learned that Christ's forgiveness in the sentence, "Father, forgive them for they know not what they do," was spoken for His persecutors around the cross. The cry is still heard today, for all of us alive to realize something of the depths of God's love and *continual forgiveness*—His kindness toward undeserving mankind. We can alter the above quotation to say...

"Kindness is continual forgiveness toward an undeserving individual."

What if you are still angry after realizing again what Jesus went through to forgive you *and your enemy?*

It's a problem of the heart as little Jason so wisely stated. Forgiveness is not enough; you need a heart.

The only heart that will do the job is not a makeover of your old carnal, sick one. You need that wonderful heart of Jesus that is bound to the Father in love and kindness. You need to experience the process of *receiving His heart at every moment of need.*

"A new heart also will I give you, and a new spirit will I put within you: and I will take away the stony heart out of your flesh, and I will give you an heart of flesh." (**Ezekiel 36:26**).

Right now while feeling battered and beaten, discouraged with yourself, and disappointed in realizing that it is still possible for old unwanted thoughts and feelings to arise again—*right this moment you may have His new heart.*

Don't ask for little thimbles-full of love and kindness; don't ask merely that the anger go away. Ask for *all of Him* to live in you. By having Him you will receive everything you need. You will be experiencing His betrothal promise of His *righteousness,* His *loving-kindness,* His *mercies,* and His *judgment*—the kind that brings about justice in your life, even His *faithfulness.* (**Hosea 2:19, 20**).

A beautiful engagement ring, a lovely hope chest, a romantic moment under a full moon can never hold a candle to an engagement promise from the King of the universe *to give you all His own attributes of character to replace the miserable ones you were born with on planet earth. From these five attributes so freely bestowed we get a more complete picture of "grace," and more of the depth of meaning in that precious word.* Watch for attributes that come in "five" throughout Scripture and think of His grace when you find them.

Even with all this, reality reminds us of those of you who have known the depths of shame and despair in a terrible past that defies understanding. Even though you've experienced God's grace in the born-again experience, the pain, the disgrace and humiliation you feel still plague you.

It may be that you suffered terrible abuse in your childhood. It may have been constant verbal put-downs, physical beating, or worse yet—sexual abuse at the hands of someone who should have been lovingly protecting your innocent childhood. Now you feel scarred for life, and impossibly ruined forever.

Here is your opportunity to shed old thinking patterns! If your past was full of pain because of someone else's evil deeds toward you, *that individual is the one to carry the scars if those deeds have never been repented of and brought to Jesus.*

Sin *does* leave scars on the victims. They show up in the baggage of psychological hang-ups, feelings of low self-worth that develop into controlling others, acting bravado, or insecure and unable to stand firm for convictions. However, *you* were *the victim,* and yes, you may have wrestled with doubts about who you are, with misperceptions of how unclean and worthless you have become after your born-again experience. You may be taking responsibility for such mishandling in childhood; you may have been viewing yourself as responsible as the perpetrator of wrong. Please look carefully at these facts about sin:

1. "Sin" describes the *nature* of a person who is carnal—*one who has not accepted God's spiritual new nature.* The "sin" nature in an unholy person dwells on impure, or evil ideas, then carries them out in harmful, hurtful actions with no care how these wrongs affect the victim.
2. Any individual, whether adult or child, held against his or her will is *a victim* of someone else's sins—those wrong acts. The *victim is not* engaged in sin, and is not guilty before God.
3. If you are a victim of violence of any kind against your body, the body is not polluted, degraded or guilty before God, although you may feel as if this is so. Your body is only polluted if your mind is polluted. Besides, in a few years *all the cells in your body are completely replaced by new ones, so you are not the same person physically, anyway.* Did I hear a Hallelujah?
4. Although you might feel temporary shame or degradation in your mind, these have been settled when Jesus shed His blood. *He forgave the perpetrator who wronged you in His prayer when He hung on the cross* and said, "Father forgive them for they know not what they do." The one who wronged you is liberated to accept that forgiveness freely offered by Christ, if led by his realization of conviction before God. Whether he ever chooses to accept that forgiveness is up to him; it is *now your turn* to also *accept His forgiveness given to this sinner.*
5. By the way, while Christ hung naked before the world, terribly wronged by the religious leaders of his day, his shame did not pollute His mind; *He carried no conviction of personal wrongs—no passion of anger.* While He became sin for us, His divine mind was never tarnished; it only made it all the more painful for Him who was pure and

holy to carry your sin and mine to the cross. He was pure as always in His sanctified humanity.

6. If you feel persistent feelings of shame and guilt, realize that this is *guilt* from the adversary the devil, and is *not* conviction of sin. It is a ploy of Satan to endeavor to make you feel shamed and discouraged. *You did not sin in being the victim, so you do not have a real reason to feel guilt.* Feelings of guilt do not bring anyone to repentance and should be thrown back in the face of Satan as untrue, and unaccepted. Praise God that you are free in Him to accept the wonderful gift of His divine mind!

Claim these two promises as yours, as real as receiving a beautifully wrapped present on your birthday.

"Let this mind be in you, which was also in Christ Jesus." **(Philippians 2:5).**

Whereby are given unto us exceeding great and precious promises: that by these *ye might be partakers of the divine nature...* **(2 Peter 1:4).**

Claim that promise as your own and thank God often that He is giving you His nature and His attitudes!

"Forasmuch then as Christ hath suffered for us in the flesh, *arm yourselves likewise with the same mind: for he that hath suffered in the flesh hath ceased from sin;* **(1 Peter 4:1).**

THOUGHT QUESTIONS:

1. Have you been born again *today? Whatever time of day it is right now, it is not too late!*

2. When you were last tempted to think the same old thoughts in the same old way, did you stop and consider that those troubles and disappointments were all really allowed from Jesus—that He feels the pain before you? When you are distressed He has come to draw you to Himself and teach you what you otherwise could not understand.

3. Did you ask for the power in His promised mind, supplanting your old thought patterns, those feelings of despair, or hopelessness? Did you thank Him for this salvation promised in Romans 5:10, that *you are saved by His life?*

4. Are you allowing Him to take the misery and pain of the past, even the deep sorrow of the long-ago, and supplant it all with moment-by-moment rejoicing in Him? Now you are free to accept any present, earthly rejection knowing Jesus claims you as His own.

Remember to praise Him every day for the new you that He is producing. Thank Him that He is giving you *His* heart, *even His very nature!*

If you are still struggling, study these lessons again, walking through the outlined steps. Choose to rejoice when you don't feel like rejoicing. Choose to allow His positive, trusting nature to replace those old, worn-out wrong ruts in the road of your mind!

2 Corinthians 10:4, 5—(For the weapons of our warfare are not carnal, but mighty through God *to the pulling down of strong holds;)*

Casting down imaginations, and every high thing that exalteth itself against the knowledge of God, and *bringing into captivity every thought* to the obedience of Christ;

Only His mind can cast down imaginations. Only His heart, transplanted in place of your carnal one, can supply His sanctified new thoughts, His own full forgiveness that loves others unconditionally! The Father "so loved the world that He gave His only son," and so loves you today that *He will continue to give Him to you* in the refreshing showers of rain in response to your prayers.

Acts 3:19–21—"Repent ye therefore, and be converted, that your sins may be blotted out, when the times of refreshing shall come from the presence of the Lord; And *He shall send Jesus Christ*, which before was preached unto you: Whom the heaven must receive until the times of restitution of all things "

Repentance—for hanging on to that old sinful nature—is accepted and that sin blotted out (Acts 3:19)—even *taken out* of your life, and transplanted with the loving heart of the Savior. Today is one of your "times of restitution" for they are available to us *constantly—even moment-by-moment times of receiving His mind, His heart of love and continual forgive-*

ness to you who for too-long has cherished your "right" to be upset and angry. Hopefully you have found that the price is too high to continue to hold onto those supposed rights. The time of restitution has come for continual forgiveness to your antagonists. You know that God forgave them from the beginning; He forgave them at the cross, and He forgives them today. *You may have His wonderful heart of forgiveness as your own; with it comes the ability to extend His forgiveness to those who wound and hurt you.*

If you feel that every injustice in your life is too big for you to forgive, you are probably right. However, remember that you cannot forgive for it is not possible for your old carnal heart to feel right or to change. Submit to His way of bringing continual victory of the past by surrendering your mind to Him at every moment of trial *until His heart of forgiveness is yours to stay. His forgiveness will be sufficient!*

Assignments

1. *You may receive His forgiving heart with a "mind transplant" and only that mind transplant will do. Surrender and submit to Him to experience the miracle of His grace—the mystery of Christ in you—the hope of glory!* (Read carefully **1 Corinthians 1 and 2**)
2. Continue claiming God's promises, and any of the projects suggested in the first 3 lessons that you have found to be helpful Make them habits!
3. Read the supplement, **You Can Have Nerve Power From the Holy Spirit.**
4. Think of the many times that Jesus comes to you each day through His Word and the comfort of the Holy Spirit, to draw you to Him, and give you strength to live for Him.

HE COMES TODAY

1. Do you long to see our Jesus come in glory?
Or hear the sound of trumpets pierce the sky?
Do you wonder just how long, 'til you hear the angels' song
Did you wait for only later, bye and bye?

2. Did you hear sweet Jesus speak to you at daybreak,
With wondrous words to heal your inmost soul?
Did you feel His presence near, did you let Him take your fear
Did you know He only wants to make you whole?

Chorus:
He comes today; don't miss the treading of His feet.
He comes today; hear His voice like music sweet
In His promise to abide, in His presence where we hide
From storms of life—our joy in Him complete. E. D.

YOU CAN HAVE NERVE POWER FROM THE HOLY SPIRIT

Yes, even when your limit of endurance seems stretched beyond reason, you can have power you may never have realized. While we consider those tough friendships, here is incredible comfort to know and receive.. Have you entered into work or friendship relationships that have surprised and saddened you? Perhaps you expected more returns in marriage, or from your grown children, siblings or classmates, maybe from your parents after you are an adult. Instead, there have been accusations, criticism, or a care less attitude that has left you stunned and heartsick. Worse yet, you've been left now to battle feelings of resentment and bitterness that threaten to take your inner born–again nature, that you commit to God each morning and replace it with those ugly, old–covenant feelings in your heart of hearts.

Then, when you tried to ask forgiveness the haranguing begins all over again. Some antagonists use your repentance as a chance to rehearse your supposed failures further, and to berate you for hours in person or on the phone, leaving you shaken and in a worse condition than before you attempted to solve the estrangement.

God's word has hope and comfort for you as well as a new way to look at your situation. You will no longer need to succumb to the overwhelming feeling of being a victim of depression or any other ploy of Satan.

Our heavenly Father looked down through the ages and spoke through the Apostle *Peter with a special victory key for you. He said...*

I Peter 1.6—Wherein ye greatly rejoice, though now for a season, if need be, ye are in heaviness through manifold temptations:

Rejoice? Rejoice when tired, upset and drained? Why should I rejoice?

Verse 7—That *the trial of your faith,* being much more precious than of gold that perisheth, *though it be tried[1381] with fire,* might be found unto praise and honor and glory at the appearing of Jesus Christ: (**1381** in Strong's Concordance means *to prove, bring forth the good (not the evil traits of our character!)*

In other words, by choosing to rejoice in the Lord, He will do something for you, in you, through you! This trial is permitted to help you develop precious traits of character that will fit you for heaven. He wants to make you a new person.

I know; you may equate rejoicing with the normal response of happy events, wonderful surprises, lessening of cares and burdens of your life. This rejoicing is not the same as excited, human responses to life's joyful moments. This is the obedient response to a Bible command. It will become Bible sanctification to you, as you learn to walk trustingly with surrender to God's will in your life. It is exercising your spiritual "soul muscles," and seeing God awaken in you a new life in Him, and in so doing you are allowing your natural, carnal heart to "die."

Romans 8:11—But if the Spirit of him that raised up Jesus from the dead dwell in you, he that raised up Christ from the dead shall also quicken your mortal bodies by his Spirit that dwelleth in you.

How else can He quicken you, if you do not die, and *how else can you die to self, if there is never a temptation presented that demands this decision from you?*
Job said something similar in the Old Testament:
Job 23:10—...When He hath *tried* me, I shall come forth as gold.
Tried—to prove, to test, examine
This is an Old Testament equivalent of the word "tried." The trial of your life, the actions of others that seem as a thorn in your side, may well be your examination, a test to allow you to see the inner you, and to learn how you do under duress! If you are feeling the "normal" or "natural" human nature feelings you will know you have some dying to self to do, but look at the reward!
Isaiah 48:10—Behold I have refined thee, but not with silver; I have chosen thee in the furnace of affliction.
Had you thought of this verse as appropriate only for those with personal physical suffering, perhaps? Are your daily stresses any less painful?
Would you like to experience peace instead of pain, or joy instead of anger and resentment? Don't try harder to keep from getting upset; it won't work. This is the moment of real growth, *when you allow the Holy Spirit to give you the gift promised by Jesus—Himself.* He wants to give you His divine nature (II Peter I: 4), that heavenly essence of the mind that Jesus possessed. It is time now to accept His New Covenant writing of the law on our hearts, bringing us to the place where we can accept His forgiveness prayed on the cross— **the forgiveness that embraced your antagonists as well as you!** You may need to repeat this submission moment by moment until the victory is fully attained.
"We have great victories to gain, and a heaven to lose if we do not gain them. The carnal heart must be crucified; for its tendency is to moral corruption, and the end thereof is death. Nothing but the life-giving influences of the gospel can help the soul. Pray that *the mighty energies of the Holy Spirit, with all their quickening, recuperative, and transforming power, may fall like an electric shock on the palsy-stricken soul, causing every nerve to thrill with new life,* restoring the whole man

from his dead, earthly, sensual state to spiritual soundness. *You will thus become partakers of the divine nature*, having escaped the corruption that is in the world through lust; and in your souls will be reflected the image of Him by whose stripes you are healed." Volume 5 of the **Testimonies to the Church**, page 267

Paul said it well in Ephesians, chapter 3:

Verse16—That he would grant you, according to the riches of his glory, *to be strengthened with might by his Spirit in the inner man;*

17—That Christ may dwell in your hearts by faith; that ye, being rooted and grounded in love,

18—May be able to comprehend with all saints what is the breadth, and length, and depth, and height;

19—And to know the love of Christ, which passeth knowledge, that ye might be filled with all the fullness of God.

What will that fullness do? It will not only supply the calm acceptance of whatever someone feels called to dish out to you, but beyond that, it will place you in the position of an intercessor for that individual. After all, hearing the accusations, the unkindness, the lack of mercy is not really about you after all; in all of this *you are learning that this individual desperately needs your prayers and your care along with your thoughtful, urgent, intercession.*

Can it be that God is using this very troubling encounter to make you aware of this desperate need? Can you be the prayer warrior for your "enemy" rather than giving the natural "piece of your mind," you **feel** like giving? Are you strong enough to be an ambassador for God instead of retreating in tears to lick your wounds? No, you are not—of yourself. Before you answer though, consider this:

> Christ's Word is the bread of life and the water of salvation. Trust in its fullness comes to us through constant communion with God. By it we gain spiritual strength. Christ supplies the life-blood of the heart, and *the Holy Spirit gives nerve power.* Begotten again unto a lively hope, imbued with the quickening power of a new nature, the soul is enabled to rise higher and still higher.—**Signs of the Times**, 1900, Volume 10, page 3.

*Think of it: **nerve power**! Just what we need! Here is your challenge; begin praising God when the going is rough as well as on calm, happy days. Show your trust in God by putting Him to the test. Give Him a chance to forever change you. Through your response to Him, let Him work out His will in the lives of others around you as well!*

Lesson 5

THROWING OFF THE SPIRIT OF HEAVINESS TO RECEIVE HIS

GARMENT OF PRAISE

"What a great day!" The crew had been helpful, with no misunderstandings to mar sweet fellowship at work. Now a short ride through the countryside would be followed by time in the garden in the evening sunshine. Nothing but positive, joyful thoughts would fill my driving time; right?

Wrong! As I turned my car onto the highway, a heavy weight enveloped and seemed to settle like a big, black blanket over my car with me trapped inside. At work my life was on display; here in my own car on a quiet, country highway, I could tell God how pointless my life really seemed, and how unimportant I felt. It might even bring relief to cry a bit and release some tension.

As soon as those thoughts came however, I knew better. I was tired from the days' activities, and needed to rest. To give way to dark feelings would only feed the enemy of souls and give him an advantage over me to needle me even more.

Instantly I made a decision; I would not even allow my face to betray my feelings. I would not cry, and I would not even plead with God for relief. Instead, I determined to sing a praise song to my loving heavenly Father. **Sing**? But I didn't *feel* like singing! Besides, my voice wasn't up to par and with this present down feeling, I knew it couldn't be trusted to bring forth anything worth listening to. But who would hear? No one but the Lord and his angels—and the enemy and his angels! I made my decision; *I will sing and declare that God is my helper* before all these unseen beings.

When I opened my mouth, out came squeaky, shaky notes that would hardly qualify as singing, but as I persisted the song became sure and strong. At the end of the verse, the

black, heavy blanket of doubt, despair, and moodiness float-
ed away as fluffy feathers before a stiff wind. In a prayer of
thankfulness, I rejoiced the rest of the way home, telling God
how much I appreciated His power in my life, and how grateful I was for making it so plain how to resist Satan when he
comes to harass and tempt to despair. What began as a sacrifice—to give up a cherished right to shed some tears, became
a victory and a restful experience in the Lord.

In these few lessons on dealing with dark days of despair,
you have honestly faced your history only long enough to
realize that wrong perceptions and real pain of your past did
not need to damage your self-image or your ability to cope
with life. You are learning to walk each day in the victories
that Jesus already won for you, submitting each little (and
bigger!) trial to Him. You are rejoicing in a freedom you may
have never experienced.

What about the future? Can your new understandings of
how to rise above the petty problems of past and present
make your mind a fortress for future troubles? No matter
what your church affiliation, or even if you believe there is
a God but belong to no church at all, you are realizing that
something is building up to a climax in this world; the world
we once knew seems very out-of-control. You are not sure
what the future holds, but you can't evade the thought that
we live in no ordinary times.

What if you become a participant of another "twin-tow-
ers" episode, and you escape only moments before a huge
collapse of a building? What if you see disasters of that mag-
nitude pile one upon another until you are firmly convinced
that this is not merely the "beginning of sorrows," but the
"great tribulation" that you always believed you would *not*
see because you would have been "raptured" secretly? What
if your understanding of the Bible is shaken to its very core
leaving you helpless and fearful with the thought that if "the
secret rapture" was not the truth, then *what is the truth*?

We have advanced to the place where we must cease talking merely about your reactions to life; we must now move
to knowing Jesus so well, to understanding and firmly believing that what He has promised He will do, that we can trust

Him fully no matter what the future holds. The only way to do that is to follow where He walked, and gain an experience beyond what you ever imagined. You can move from simply *surviving* in this world of sorrow and degradation, to *thriving* in your daily walk, prepared and confident of His presence and His power.

You can begin by receiving a long-ago promise to Moses concerning His people Israel as if spoken to you today,

Exodus 33:14—"My presence shall go with thee, and I will give thee rest."

That promise is for you as much as it was for the Israelites of long ago. How can you come to the place where an awesome quotation like the following will speak comfort to your heart as forcefully as if Christ should appear to you in a vision and state it plainly with a printed copy placed in your hands?

"The Father's presence encircled Christ, and *nothing befell Him but that which infinite love permitted for the blessing of the world.* Here was His source of comfort, and it is for us. He who is imbued with the Spirit of Christ, abides in Christ. *The blow that is aimed at him falls upon the Savior who surrounds him with his presence.* <u>Whatever comes to him comes from Christ.</u> He has no need to resist evil for Christ is his defense. *Nothing can touch him except by our Lord's permission, and 'all things' that are permitted 'work together for good to them that love God.'"* ***Thoughts from the Mount of Blessing,*** page 71 (**Romans 8:28**).

How can a loving God permit little children to die, or terrible calamities take precious family or friends from you, leaving you with a breaking heart?

If you have learned to trust Him in daily troubles, you will also trust Him with those lives, lost to this earth but safe in His eternal plan if they loved Him, or knowing that more probationary time would not bring them closer to Him nor change hard hearts. *You will believe that everything has touched Jesus first in your heart as truth, simply by accepting it at face value, and applying it daily to every small, real or imagined slight, and every hurtful physical event that Satan attempts to use against you.* Whether accidents, loss of home or other real goods, or bodily harm, you will recognize that God is feeling your loss and pain. You will take every discouraging, unkind, thoughtless, disrespectful, maligning word that comes to you and realize that it is permitted by a loving God to test and prove you—to show that you trust Him. You will take a moment to fasten your mind on the truth that *this ugly thing must have gone through Him first.* You will refuse to allow your old carnal nature to breed feelings of resentment, injustice, selfishness, martyrdom, or any other "self" issue. *You will tell Jesus that you are thankful that He bore the brunt of this pain back at the cross as keenly as if it were today, and surrender all your supposed "rights" to feel wounded, neglected or forgotten by Him. You will recognize that you are experiencing a special oneness with Christ as you choose to suffer for His sake.*

At any moment of threatened despair, *He burns out any selfish thought in you and puts His mind in your mind; you become a modern day firewalker—and you are not burned! As you surrender your carnal nature to Him, He replaces your old thoughts and feelings* of resentment, selfishness, and "poor me," *with* His forgiveness, love, and compassion for others and you surrender yourself to the God of the universe who must do His work in the way He knows best. As you surrender those old, wrong thinking habit patterns to Him, *that Spirit of burning does its work at that moment, burning out all the "self" issues with nothing left but His glory—His character, with those graces of the Spirit befitting of a true Christian. You find yourself prepared to minister to others for now you know that...*

Instead of the Spirit of...	He gives His promised spirit of...
fear (II Timothy 1:7)	power and love (II Timothy 1:7)
haste (Proverbs 14:29)	patience (Ecclesiastes 7:8)
troubled (John 14:1) or unbelief (Hebrews 3:12)	belief + trust = faith (John 1:14)
hopelessness (Ephesians 2:12)	grace & supplications (Zecharia 12:10)
jealousy (Proverbs 6:34)	oneness or unity (I Corinthians 6:17)

Instead of the Spirit of...	He gives His promised spirit of...
haughty or proud (Proverbs 16:18)	humble (Proverbs 16:19)
error (I John 4:6)	truth (John 14:17)
sorrow (Psalms 13:2)	joy & rejoicing (Jeremiah 15:16)

We can add one more unwanted spirit to that list with its precious counterpart. It is a miracle of His grace when you can let this one go, even in the face of a terrific tsunami, a violent hurricane with loved ones missing in its wake, or an earthquake that leaves your home ruined beyond repair.

That miracle happens when He replaces the spirit of...

• heaviness (Isaiah 61:3) with the
• garment of praise (Hebrews 13:15)
• and know that "he hath covered (you) with His
• robe of righteousness" (Isaiah 61:10).

Yes, you will need to *choose* praise, but as you claim the promise in Isaiah 61 verse 3, and Hebrews 13:15, you find the Savior doing that work in you.

Hebrews 13:15—"By him therefore let us offer *the sacrifice of praise* to God continually, that is, the fruit of our lips *giving thanks to his name.*

Isaiah 61:3—To appoint unto them that mourn in Zion, to give unto them beauty for ashes, *the oil of joy for mourning, the garment of praise for the spirit of heaviness;* that they might be called trees of righteousness, the planting of the LORD, that he might be glorified.

Praise will be in your mouth when you walk through the fires and are not burned even as Shadrach, Meshack and Abednego were not burned long ago on the plain of Dura. Why is this so? Because, like those faithful young men, you will find yourself walking with the Son of God! Awesome!

Assignments:

1. You have read it in this lesson, now it is time to make it all your own. Take the promises on page 48, and write them on cards for easy memorization. Jot the offending negative spirit on the reverse side to remind yourself that you are fighting that specific wrong spirit *with a promised right spirit from heaven.* Memorize these promises, and thank God for

specific ones when tempted with the old negative reactions to life's tough moments.

2. Read Psalm 91, and thank your heavenly Father that He is enabling you to stand firm and strong no matter what distressing things are going on around you. You will be abiding "in the secret place of the Most High." This whole Psalm is your special promise of His presence during escalating, end-time troubles to come immediately before the second coming of Jesus in the clouds of heaven. You will not look forward with dread to that time but with joy and confidence that you have already chosen to live in His kingdom of righteousness and peace. The reality of living with Him forever is right before you—beginning NOW!

Pray this Prayer: "Father, thank You for ministering to my heart so powerfully. Thank You for supplying Your forgiveness and compassion to me and for giving me the compassionate heart of Jesus. I thank You that You are providing me with Your feelings of compassion and love to others even if they hurt me. May I never forget that whatever pain I feel, You feel it first. Keep me strong; keep me close to you moment by moment that when a spirit of heaviness threatens to cloud my day, I will offer a sacrifice of praise instead. May there be no catastrophe big enough, no sorrow so deep as to put a wedge between my heart and Yours. In the precious name of Jesus, and because of His blood shed for me, Amen."

"Rejoice in the Lord always and again I say rejoice!" (Philippians 4:4).

THE AWESOME TRUTH ABOUT GOD'S FIRE

A Bible Study

Perhaps you've thought of God's fire as something unwanted—a thing to dread. You may have heard of hellfire, and sought to escape that fire by a trip to the altar during a moving sermon at your church.

Yes, it's true; a final fire *is* coming; no doubt about it—a fire reserved for the devil and his angels. (**Matthew 25:41**). It will also forever burn up evil in every form and any sinners who choose to treasure wickedness. They will cease to exist—be only "ashes under your feet," so we know *that final fire will at last go out and sin and sinners will be no more.* (**Malachi 4:1–3**) Thank God for His mercy! He is not a God who would keep those fires burning forever—only *the effects of that fire are everlasting!*

But did you know that God's fires are burning now as well?

1. Where do the fires of God originate? _____
   _____(**Daniel 7:10**).
2. The messages of 3 angels includes the sentence, "The hour of *His judgment is* _____." (**Revelation 14:7**) Not *will come* someday, but *is come.* The word judgment here means "separation or sundering from sin." This suggests a portion of God's judgment before the final sentencing—a time when the great judge of the earth acts as a mediator to prepare His own people to avoid the final fires.
3. What cleansing words in Malachi 3:3 shows what God is doing on His throne during heavenly cleansing of His people? (**Malachi 3:3**)_____ _____.
4. Man's work shall not only be _____by fire, (**I Corinthians 3:13**) but also _____by fire as well. (**I Corinthians 3:15**).

5. The people of God are not only refined by the Spirit of
   _____but also by the Spirit of _____
   _____. (**Isaiah 4:4**).

6. Finally, what are these fire walkers called? _____
   _____What goes before them and behind them?___
   _____(**Joel 2:2**).

7. To what else are God's people likened?_____
   _____(**Isaiah 5:1–7**).

8. What is God's sorrowful lament in **Isaiah 5:4**—" What
   more could I have done for my _____that I
   have not_____in it?"

9. The answer to His question is not given fully in chapter
   5 of Isaiah. He picks up the theme again in **Isaiah 27:
   2**. "In that day sing ye unto her, A _____ of
   _____ _____." Red = the color of blood;
   wine = new doctrine. We might wonder what a "doctrine
   involving the blood of Christ" would do.

10. God is full of zeal here for His precious church. In
    verse 4 He describes His actions to save his church. He
    says, "Who would set the _____ and _____ against
    me in battle? I would go through them, **I would burn them
    together**." Briers and thorns = _____ (**Isaiah
    33:12**) Notice *He is not going to burn His vineyard*, but only
    the briers and thorns-those with the attitudes and actions
    of the devil who seeks to bring us to sin and shame. That
    is real judgment without a shred of judgmentalism from
    people that we experience so often today.

11. How do we know that His fire can be to us a good fire
    when we read verses such as **Nahum 1:6**? "Who can
    stand before his indignation? and who can _____ in the
    _____of his anger? His _____ is poured out like
    _____, and the rocks are thrown down by him."

12. We can know that we are safe in times of trouble by His
    promises: "The LORD is good, a _____ _____ in the
    day of trouble; and he knoweth _____ that _____in
    him." (**Nahum 1:7**).

13. What brings us to this trusting relationship? You will find
    it in **Isaiah 27:3**—"I the LORD do keep it; (His vineyard!)
    I will _____ it every _____: lest any _____it,

I will keep it night and day." Water represents the Holy Spirit of God—that special outpouring of Himself to bring comfort, healing and power to bless others at the end of time.

14. Why is all this cleansing now important? What will it do for and in us? (**1 Corinthians 3:13**) "Every man's work shall be _____ _____...for it shall be revealed by _____"

15. More than this, you will come to regard it as a privilege to be "bearing about in the body the _____ of the Lord Jesus (that's the surrender of self!), that the _____ also of Jesus might be _____ _____ in our body. For we which live are _____ delivered unto _____ (to self) for Jesus' sake, that the _____also of _____ might be made manifest in _____mortal flesh." (**2 Corinthians 4:10, 11**). What a joy! To show the world what Jesus is like, even as Jesus came to show the character of the Father.

16. If you've taken the lessons in this book to heart, you've been watered moment by moment. You've been preparing yourself for that glorious rain of His Spirit that will eclipse any glorious outpouring of His grace ever experienced on this earth. It is described in **Hosea 6:3**—"Then shall we know, if we _____ on to know the LORD: his going forth is prepared as the morning; and He shall come unto us as the _____, as the _____ and _____rain unto the earth." (See also **Joel 2:23–32**; **James 5:6, 7**)

17. One more thing; just what is this "fire" of God that is doing the cleansing work in you and in me today? (**Psalms 79:5**)—"How long, LORD? wilt thou be **angry** for ever? shall thy _____ burn like _____?"

Remember the second commandment? "For I the Lord thy God am a *jealous* God...(**Exodus 20:5**)

He is jealous for you for He has claimed you as His own. He is a jealous Lover doing everything He can to get your attention, to bring you into His own heart of love, to shelter you in His stronghold. He is a jealous Father who sent His only Son to rescue you from the effects of sin and from the sin itself.

Beyond surviving in this world of pain and sorrow, if you've positively responded to the five major steps in the pages of this book, you possess the *keys to thriving* in spite of all the hard knocks of your life. You are now learning to trust this loving God who created you to live forever. You are knowing Him, *not as a fire escape*, but the place of peace described in **Revelation 15:2**—"And I saw as it were *a sea of glass mingled with fire*: and *them that had gotten the victory...*" No, this is *not* describing heaven! The setting is the time of *the seven last plagues*, the last few months of earth time. It describes a people who have learned to trust God—those who are modern-day fire walkers. They have found that the safest, most peaceful place to stay is around God's throne, fiery though it may be, for they appreciate being rid of inherited tendencies to sin, and from cultivated unChristlike habits!

Are *YOU* staying in the fire around the throne of God— thankful that He is watering you with His Spirit, every moment?

GLORY TO JESUS
(In a walk through the Sanctuary)

Glory—to Jesus my King—
For He is the reason my heart can sing –
of His grace to save me from sin's dark shame
Oh how I praise Him because He came
from heaven to earth below

Ps 57:5; Isa 42:12; Luke 2:14
Ps 13:5,6; Ps 51:14, Ps. 33:3
I Cor 15:34 (altar of sacrifice)

Luke 23:46 **to the courtyard—
the altar representing the cross**

**Washed by His Word every morning
Cleansed by his blood applied
Born of His Spirit, igniting my soul**

Keeping me close to His side.

Eph 5:2 Table of Shewbread
Lev. 14:4
**John 3:5,6; John 10:10 (I, as one
Lamp in the lampstand—His church.)**
John 14:15—comforter—"One who
comes along beside."

Glory—to Jesus my King
For He is the reason my heart can sing
of His power to grant me His life—His mind,

Ps 24:8; Ps 84:11; Heb 13:21
Ps 7:17
Col 1:11; 1 Pet 1:5; Rev 18:1;
Jn 3:16, Phil 2:5 **(Table of
Shewbread—continually claiming
His promises Moment by moment!)**

In Him my joy and His vic'try I find
Filling my inmost soul.

Heb 1:9; Heb 2: 11, 21; I Jn 1:7; 1 Jn 1:9, Eph 5:26; 2 Cor 7:1

**Boldly to God's place of mercy,
Not for myself alone,**

**Heb 4:16 Altar of Incense
I Pet. 1:22; Gal 6:2
reigning with Him as a priest**
I Thess 4:9; John 15:12; Rom 12:10

Bringing the souls He has laid on my heart.

For Christ's own blood to atone.

Lev. 17:11, Heb. 9:10,11 now—the Day of Atonement

Glory--to Jesus my King

Ps 63:2; Ps 64:10; 1 Pet. 5:10, 11; Ps 21:13;

for He is the reason my heart can sing
of His love's anointing, prepared to stand,

Ps 23:5; I John 2:27; 2 Cor 1:21; Heb 3:14
Rev 19:8, Rev 17:14

Reigning with Him in redemption's plan,
Serving as priest and king.

Acts 26:6,7; I Thes 1:9; Rom 7:26 Our place with Him in the Sanctuary of His presence and our heart.

—Ellen Dana

STEPS TO INTIMATE FELLOWSHIP
WITH JESUS

1. *We have a precious promise;* The LORD hath appeared of old unto me, saying, Yea, I have loved thee with an everlasting love: therefore *with lovingkindness have I drawn thee.* (**Jeremiah 31:3**). *And He never ceases that drawing unless we persistently resist Him.*
2. *We need only to come to Him, as we are.* Jesus said, "Verily, verily, I say unto thee, Except a man be born again, he cannot see the kingdom of God. (**John 3:3**).
3. *We may not see or feel it, but the work is done in us if we ask Him.* Marvel not that I said unto thee, Ye must be born again. The wind bloweth where it listeth, and thou hearest the sound thereof, but canst not tell whence it cometh, and whither it goeth: so is every one that is born of the Spirit. (**John 3:7, 8**).
4. *When we allow Him to bring us to this born again experience, our Father God walks His courts and sings.* The LORD thy God in the midst of thee is mighty; He will save, He will rejoice over thee with joy...**He will joy over thee with singing**. (**Zephaniah 3:17**)
5. *At that moment, if we die, the full grace of Jesus saves us eternally. If we continue living, we have the awesome privilege to have a part in the changes He wants to put into effect in our lives so that we can experience the closeness to our Lord that He wants to have with us—a little foretaste of heaven.* "For we ourselves also were sometimes foolish, disobedient, deceived, serving divers lusts and pleasures, living in malice and envy, hateful, and hating one another. But after that the kindness and love of God our Savior toward man appeared, *Not by works of righteousness which we have done,* but *according to His mercy* he saved us, *by the washing of regeneration,* and *renewing of the Holy Ghost;* (**Titus 3:3–5**).

6. *This work is done through washing—first the external washing by baptism, then the daily moment by moment cleansing through the application of the principles of righteousness that we learn and experience through reading His Word.* That he might sanctify and cleanse it with *the washing of water by the word,* (**Ephesians 5:26**).

7. *We may think at times that people are the source of our problems; this is not so.* For *we wrestle not against flesh and blood,* but against *principalities,* against *powers,* against the *rulers of the darkness of this world,* against *spiritual wickedness in high places. As preparation against these "rulers of darkness," these "powers," we must put on our defense armor:* (See **Ephesians 6:13–18**)

8. *If we've done all of this, why then are there still failures? The heart is deceitful* above all things, and desperately wicked: who can know it? (**Jeremiah 17:9**).

9. *Who only really knows our hearts? I the LORD* search the heart, *I try the reins, (or the conscience, our innermost thoughts)* even to give every man according to his ways, and according to the fruit of his doings. (**Jeremiah 17:10**). *If God knows what is in us that is unlovely, thoughtless, unkind, impure, and wicked, He knows that we too, need to know. Trials help us recognize what areas we must let Him to do His work in us.*

10. *Through these trials of life, even our failures, we can see into our heart and know how hopeless is our condition to live a consistent, loving Christ-like life—except by one means—to receive His mind, His attitudes, His desires, His divine nature which is neither like Adam before or after the fall—only like divinity.* Let this mind be in you, which was also in Christ Jesus: (**Philippians 2:5—See also II Peter 1:4**).

11. *Receiving His mind is also likened to allowing God to write His law on our hearts—a promise made over and over throughout Scripture:* This is the covenant that I will make with them after those days, saith the Lord, I will put my laws into their hearts, and in their minds will I write them. (**Hebrews 10:16—**See also **Hebrews 9:6** and **Jeremiah 31: 34**)

12. *Yes, we are told to strive--Strive to enter in* at the strait gate: (**Luke 13:24**).

13. *But don't miss what **that one job or "work;"** is; it is submission to Him so that He can put His mind in our minds, <u>and wrap us up in Himself</u>:* Submit yourselves therefore to God. Resist the devil, and he will flee from you. *Humble yourselves in the sight of the Lord, and He shall lift you up.* (**James 4:7, 10**). *Resist by submitting, running quickly to His victory.*

14. *And yes, we are told to put on the "whole armor of God"* (**Ephesians 6:13–18**), *but a careful study will show that every piece of that armor represents Jesus and His righteousness. So, we've asked for His mind to be in us, now we ask that we be wrapped up in Him as well, clothed in His clothing that He provides for the wedding feast—even our character.* (**Matthew 22:11–13**) *He is not only our hope and innermost desire;* (**Psalms 37:4**) *He is our armor against Satan's assaults.* (**Ephesians 6:11–18**).

15. This is the way that you "work out your own salvation with fear and trembling." *You tremblingly submit* to the work He has promised to do! (**Philippians 2:12**).

16. *Instead of dreading each temptation and wondering if we will not "make it" this time and fall again into sin, we will recognize that this is appointment time with Jesus—the time above all times when He is close by to work His work of grace in us described above.* "To such as keep his covenant, (*The* **New Covenant of Jeremiah 31:33 and Hebrews 10:16**) and to those that remember his **commandments** to do them." (**Psalms 103:18**); (*The word commandment in this verse means "to appoint, or have an appointment with." He takes the responsibility again—as long as we submit!*)

17. *As we continue this new and exciting daily walk with our Father, we find that we* "Draw nigh to God, and He will draw nigh to you."—*We feel and experience a closeness that we cherish. It becomes easier every day to let Him fulfill the rest of that verse—*"Cleanse your hands, ye sinners; and purify your hearts, ye double minded. (**James 4:8**).

18. *It is only* **His faithfulness** *that we can trust, not ours-- only* **His faithfulness** *to finish the work He has begun in us, that we can hold onto with confidence.* Let us hold fast the profession of our faith without wavering; for He is faithful that promised; (**Hebrews 10:23).**

19. *And now the most precious of His promises:* Being *confident* of this very thing, that **He** which hath begun a good work in you *will perform it* until the day of Jesus Christ: (**Philippians 1:6).**

HE CAME...WE CAME

JESUS...(Matt. 1:21; John 17:3,4; John 1:11; John 6:38; Isa. 53)
He came to earth—without a thought of self, bereft of
    throne,
Sent by God on "Mission Earth" from royalty and Home's
adoring angels, glories yet unknown by man
Descended here to show the Father's love—Redemption's
    plan
His birth announced by heavenly angel choir
Yet subject oft each day to Satan's ire.
Ambassador from heaven's bliss, to live in much-degraded
    human skin
His mind as firmly fixed on God as Adam's before sin.
He lived His life—God's life—in every thought and deed,
Sharp contrast to our own great, every-moment need.
Yes, Jesus came to demonstrate godlikeness—showed the
    way
Of faithfulness to God each moment of the day.
That faithfulness, preserved intact in His own precious
    mind
Always close to Father—linked to ways unselfish, kind
Bequeathed to man a picture of His Father's face
As He brought down to planet earth, the *Kingdom of His*
    grace.
WE CAME...(Jer. 31:3; John 17:18; 2 Cor. 5:20; 2 Cor. 4:10,11;
    John 20:21)

We came to earth—from one small thought in God's own mind,
Conceived by loving heart long ages back in time
We too, were sent into this world of sin to show His power
to live in human life, before probation's final hour
Bereft of perfect mind as held by Christ on earth
But subject to receive His stainless Mind, in new and potent birth. (Phil 2:5; John 3:7)
And so, through us Christ lives again in evil land
Like Him, surrounded here by Satan's rebel band.
These wicked hosts would wish God's earthly saints to quake
We will not fear—*His faithfulness* we every moment take,
For Satan, "Prince Accuser," was at Calvary cast down.
When we with trust accept redemption's royal crown (Ps. 103:4)
of tender mercy, kindness—heaven's warm connection
Joined close to work with Christ in intimate affection,
For now with Jesus, Lord of all, *revealing Him—salvation's story* (**Col. 1:27**)
Ambassadors of Him we praise, with living proof, *the Kingdom of His glory*.

"As the message of Christ's *first advent* announced **the kingdom of His grace**, so the *message of His second advent* announces **the kingdom of His glory**." ***Desire of Ages***, 234 *We are the ones to give that glory by our words and by our lives!*

**Are you letting Him accomplish in you
what He brought you to earth to do?**

75

MUSIC TO POEMS IN THIS BOOK

Six of the poems included in these pages are songs composed by the author of this book. They are: **Sealed for Eternity, Because He Loves Me, Sufficiency in Him, Fill My Hand, He Comes Today,** and **Glory to Jesus**. They are beautifully rendered in keyboard and voice with non-contemporary music you won't forget.

You may own one of tшese heart-touching CD's for a donation of $8 which includes shipping. Order from Caring Communications, P.O. Box 87, Days Creek, Oregon 97429

We invite you to view the complete
selection of titles we publish at:

www.TEACHServices.com

or write or email us your praises,
reactions, or thoughts about this
or any other book we publish at:

TEACH Services, Inc.
P.O. Box 954
Ringgold, GA 30736

info@TEACHServices.com

Finally, if you are interested in seeing
your own book in print, please contact us at

publishing@teachservices.com.

We would be happy to review your manuscript for free.

www.ingramcontent.com/pod-product-compliance
Lightning Source LLC
Chambersburg PA
CBHW060441090426
42733CB00011B/2357